Advance Praise for

Being Young and Homeless

"This is an impressive book on one of the most important topics in international child welfare—homeless youth. Dr. Karabanow has thoroughly researched the process by which children become homeless and has carefully assessed the means by which they can be recovered. Highly recommended."

Mark Lusk, Associate Provost for International Affairs,
The University of Georgia, USA

"A must read for anyone who wants to make a difference in the lives of street involved youth. *Being Young and Homeless: Understanding How Youth Enter And Exit Street Life*, puts the reader on the street and offers huge insights into the crisis of youth homelessness and the real solutions."

Angela Bishop, Halifax Community Action on Homelessness

BEING YOUNG AND HOMELESS

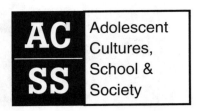

Joseph L. DeVitis & Linda Irwin-DeVitis
GENERAL EDITORS

Vol. 30

PETER LANG
New York • Washington, D.C./Baltimore • Bern
Frankfurt am Main • Berlin • Brussels • Vienna • Oxford

Jeff Karabanow

BEING YOUNG AND HOMELESS

Understanding How Youth Enter and Exit Street Life

PETER LANG
New York • Washington, D.C./Baltimore • Bern
Frankfurt am Main • Berlin • Brussels • Vienna • Oxford

Library of Congress Cataloging-in-Publication Data

Karabanow, Jeff.
Being young and homeless: understanding how
youth enter and exit street life / Jeff Karabanow.
p.   cm. — (Adolescent cultures, school & society; v. 30)
Includes bibliographical references and index.
1. Homeless youth—Canada. 2. Homeless youth—Guatemala—Guatemala.
3. Homeless youth—Services for—Canada. 4. Homeless youth—Services for—
Guatemala—Guatemala. 5. Street youth—Canada. 6. Street youth—
Guatemala—Guatemala. I. Title. II. Series.
HV4509.K37   362.7'086'942—dc22   2004001655
ISBN 0–8204–6781–2
ISSN 1091–1464

Bibliographic information published by **Die Deutsche Bibliothek**.
Die Deutsche Bibliothek lists this publication in the "Deutsche
Nationalbibliografie"; detailed bibliographic data is available
on the Internet at http://dnb.ddb.de/.

Cover design by Dutton & Sherman Design

Contents

Acknowledgments   vii

CHAPTER ONE
Introduction   1
The who of street youth: How we talk about them   2
Major tenets of the book   4
Methodology   6
Why this book?   8

CHAPTER TWO
A History of Homelessness in Western Society:
From the Spiritual Wanderer to the Squeegee Kid   10
Historical responses to homelessness   12
Homeless youth in history   16
Who are the present-day homeless?   20
Adult homelessness   21
Adult shelters   23

CHAPTER THREE
Where Do They Come From? The Etiology of Street Youth   26
Why kids run   26
Etiological factors   28
Street youth and the child welfare system   32

CHAPTER FOUR

The Long and Winding Road: La Rue, La Calle, and the Street   38

Common challenges   40

Street life as a career   46

Pre-entry conditions   47

Contemplation   50

Home is where you make it: Entering street culture   53

Building identity   58

Disengagement/exiting street culture   62

Agency and street careers   68

CHAPTER FIVE

Who's Helping? A Look at Organizational Responses to Street Youth   69

The youth shelter   69

Health services and street youth   72

School and street youth   73

Alternatives   74

Mapping what works   77

Locality development   77

Social development   80

Active participation   82

Structural definition of situation   85

Consciousness raising   86

Social action   87

Conceptual frameworks   88

CHAPTER SIX

Conclusion   90

Resilience and courage   90

Alternative systems   91

Merging locality development and social action   92

Lessons from the field   93

Notes   95

Bibliography   99

Acknowledgments

This book represents a culmination of my clinical work and research endeavors over the decade with various street youth populations in various urban landscapes. There are many people who have guided my work and opened doors to specific arenas which would have proven more difficult without their guidance. Dr. Prue Rains and Dr. Eli Teram were significant mentors to my academic activities—showing me the importance of responsible, authentic, respectful, and honest scholarship—I thank them both for this. Street youth organizations such as Covenant House, Dans La Rue, Phoenix Youth Services, ARK, and Casa Alianza went out of their way to allow me to investigate the inner workings of their organizations as well as the street experiences of their residents/participants—without their support this book could not have been written. Equally important are the many street youth who shared intimate and revealing accounts of their young lived journeys—signaling their courage, resilience and stamina in the face of much adversity—I am truly indebted to them and truly amazed by their survival skills. I would like to also thank Dr. Cassandra Hanrahan for her thoughtful and thorough review of my work and her remarkable skill in bringing together many of my dispersed thoughts in a much clearer fashion.

To Lan and Ethan, you are my world and I am deeply indebted to your uncompromising love and support during the writing journey. I dedicate this work to you.

CHAPTER ONE

Introduction

. . . To the rest of the city [Cornerville] is a mysterious, dangerous and depressing area. Respectable people have access to a limited body of information about Cornerville . . . People appear as social work clients, as defendants in criminal cases, or as undifferentiated members of the "masses". . . There is one thing wrong with such a picture: no human beings are in it.
Whyte, 1955:xv

The well-known American sociologist William Whyte highlights an important limitation in how we, in the Western world, understand social phenomena. By labeling specific individuals as "delinquents," "criminals," "victims," or "clients," we fail to see them as human beings. Typically, the social services designed to help those designated people also fail. My research here, along with that of others, confirms the reality that the social programs successful in attracting and helping street youth are those which have provided real places where these adolescents feel safe, cared for, and part of a community. Such conditions in turn make possible the development of symbolic spaces in which youth service-users can, for the first time for some, begin to imagine and dream of better futures. Such programs are said to create a culture of hope—an environment in which young people gain strength, courage, resiliency, and optimism regarding present and future endeavors (Karabanow, 2003). Within the culture of hope, the notion of citizenship rather than pathology is encouraged. As one young girl staying at a Montreal street agency eloquently noted: "When I'm here, I feel like a human being; when I leave, I feel like a street kid."

A telling portrait of how well a society is performing can be obtained by exploring the lives of its children. This book investigates the present day experiences of young people on the street in four separate localities where I have had first-hand contact and opportunities to conduct research with homeless youth. Between 1991 and 2003 I have both studied and worked in the areas of social work and youth homelessness in the three Canadian cities of Montreal, Toronto, and Halifax, and in Guatemala City where I also made a film documentary about the challenges facing street children.[1] While each of the four locations has a unique political, economic, and social environment, they contain strikingly similar characteristics regarding youth homelessness.[2] In today's globalized, ever-changing world, more and more people continue to have fewer resources with which to negotiate and make sense of the rapid pace of technological developments or of our sound-bite culture. All around the world, in both developed and Third World countries, we are witnessing massive waves of homelessness, increased levels of poverty, growing disparities between low and high income groups, rising unemployment, and related dysfunctions including drug and alcohol addiction and individual, familial, and cultural violence (Campfens, 1997).

The who of street youth: How we talk about them

Youth make up over 25% of the homeless population (Cauce et al., 2000; Moncrieff, 2001). Homeless youth have been characterized as the next generation to become homeless adults[3] (Baum and Burnes, 1993). As such, in 1988 Kozol suspected we would never be able to build prisons fast enough to hold all the angry children homeless shelters were missing and/or failing. Significantly, the majority of research on street youth from the past several decades has associated homeless youth with theories about "running away" from horrors related to the family: sexual and/or physical abuse; neglect; divorce; separation; new siblings and stepparents; and general dysfunction.

While such characterizations do resonate with many, a fundamental aim of this book is to underscore the complexity of street youth populations. Street culture and street youth populations alike are comprised of many groups. In the past fifteen to twenty years investigators began using distinctions based on the quality and length of time one spent on the street, such as, for example, "in and outers," "runners," and "hard-core," in their characterizations of the homeless (Kufeldt and Nimmo, 1987; Morrisette and McIntyre, 1989; van der Ploeg, 1989). Still other classifications have arisen in the last ten years. Some, like "child welfare kids," "group home kids," and "refugees or immigrants," depict the places street youth inhabit, while others emphasize both real and apparent practices of street youth, using such monikers as "squeegee kids," "prostitutes," "druggies," and "gang-bangers" (Karabanow, 2000; McCarthy, 1990; Shane, 1989). More recently, another important distinction has been made between kids "on the street" and kids "of the street" (Green, 1998; Lusk, 1992; Ortiz de Carrizosa and Poertner, 1992; Panter-Brick and Smith, 2000; Raffaelli, 1997)—this taxonomy in particular, describes youth who make the street their home, while the former suggests some youth only work and play on the street, returning to their family dwellings to sleep (this is especially the case, for instance, in Latin American cities).

In so far as categorical labels do describe some aspects of street youth culture, they are nonetheless partial, frequently limiting our understanding of street youth as diversified complex people. It is imperative to recognize what purposes labels serve, whom they are meant to serve and how they, all too often, do a disservice to their designates, while ostensibly facilitating the work of researchers and policy makers. Youth prostitutes, for example, do not only prostitute. Prostitution is typically a means of survival and can be often connected to other particular habits, such as an addiction. Similarly, homeless youth may in fact have homes or access to an address. Street youth are generally understood in the more progressive academic literature and in the social work practice field as adolescents who earn their livelihood by working on the streets or who reside on the streets full or part-time (Lusk, Peralta, and Vest, 1989). For the purposes of this research, I define a street youth as any young person (generally between the ages of eleven and twenty-one) who does not have a permanent place to call home, and who instead spends a significant amount of time on the street, which is to say, in alleyways, parks, storefronts, and dumpsters, among many other places; in squats (located usually in abandoned buildings); at youth shelters and centers; and/or with friends (typically referred to as "couch surfers").

Unlike previously established taxonomies, this definition removes the focus from etiology and illegal and/or unconventional activities by homeless adolescents. Instead, by encompassing a broad range of places frequented by street youth, this description functions as the framework for my overall analysis, which attempts to pull together common themes that have arisen from the experiences of diverse groups of young people living in diverse street settings.

Major tenets of the book

The scope of this study encompasses my clinical practice and applied research at Toronto's Covenant House (CH), Montreal's Dans La Rue (DLR) and Guatemala's Casa Alianza (CA), in addition to a recent investigation exploring salient issues for street youth in Halifax, Canada, funded by Human Resources Development Canada. Four major themes emerged in the course of my research, helping to guide my analyses and, ultimately, contributing to the structure of this book.

First, the majority of street youth are running *away* from problematic situations rather than running *toward* the street. This fundamental finding points to the imperative need for any study on homelessness to incorporate the personal experiences and voices of the homeless in order to unearth the roots of their present situations. Participants in each of the research sites revealed histories of one or more of the following: family dysfunction and/ or breakdown; problematic child welfare experiences; physical/sexual/ emotional abuse, and severe poverty. For children and youth with such adverse backgrounds the street becomes a safe haven.

Second, street life combines seemingly contradictory experiences and emotions of both security and insecurity. Paradoxically, regarding their contact with other street people, respondents frequently spoke optimistically about "community" or "family," while acknowledging at the same time their fears, distrust, and the existence of exploitation within street culture. It is this dichotomy which adds to the complexity of street culture.

Third, street youth are generally remarkably resilient. Their survival alone testifies to the strength and courage street youth exhibit in their efforts to eke out a living with little or no support and few resources. On a base level, simply the fact that these young people made the bold move to escape troubled and dangerous living arrangements attests to such strengths and motivations. For most, the street is understood as a healthier space than their past settings.

Finally, despite the increasing popularity of neoconservative values and neoliberal economics which characterize more and more environments, a number of human service organizations exemplify passionate and brave commitments to building a social safety net. Such nongovernmental community-based centers continue to function in face of greater advocacy for less government in the market place, and for the replacement of state care with community care. Increasingly, nonprofit organizations and the workers who manage them are the sole players "in the trenches" or on the "front line"—repairing, controlling, and defending various populations. This phenomenon was described several years ago by Jeremy Rifkin in his well-known study of community development:

> Community based organizations will increasingly act as arbiters and ombudsmen with the large forces of the marketplace and government, serving as the primary advocates and agents of social and political reform. Third-sector organizations are also likely to take up the task of providing more and more basic services in the wake of cutbacks in government aid and assistance to persons and neighborhoods in need. (1995:249)

The organizational cases used in this analysis are representative of how voluntary, nonprofit organizations have become the primary providers of particular services, while the government has, through contracting, become a purveyor of funds.

This book, therefore, is also about the privatization of social welfare in its most common manifestation—contracting. Privatization is the process of selling off government assets such as national airlines or postal services to members of the private sector, a pecuniary process euphemistically referred to as load shedding. Within the context of the social welfare system, and as it is referred to here, contracting is the practice in which social services are funded by the government using public monies, but are implemented and/or delivered by either profit or nonprofit agents and agencies in the private sector. According to American social scientist Joel Handler (1996), contracting is the "allocation of control" from the public to the private sector. Significantly, in both industrialized and Third World nations the modus operandus of governments during the past several decades has been that of privatization or, in other words, the rejection of statism.

Generally speaking, privatization is defended ideologically by both conservatives on the right and by liberals on the left of the political spectrum, each camp ostensibly concerned with the empowerment of the citizenry.

Within the realm of social welfare, it is contested, however, whether clients "gain power" through privatization. In certain instances, privatization has simply meant a "new master" for subordinate groups with little else different (Handler, 1996:5). As such, how services are delivered may be more important than who delivers them (Kramer, 1994:44). Therefore, when it comes to the (perceived) dilemma of social welfare, privatization concerns the management or diffusion of conflict, enabling those nearest to the "problem" at the local level to provide the appropriate services. As such, my analysis sheds light upon some of the organizational characteristics which appear to be successful in attracting street-entrenched youth.

Methodology

The main goal of this book is to explore the stories and struggles of children and youth living on the street, in addition to highlighting some of the programs that are successful in supporting and empowering this marginalized and, all too often, misconstrued population.

The methodology I employed in conducting my research falls under the rubric of naturalistic inquiry—combining grounded theory and ethnography. While each promotes specific techniques for understanding the social world, these naturalistic modes of inquiry are not mutually exclusive. Ethnographic research, for instance, relies heavily on the qualitative approach of participant observation. A researcher must become "immersed in the field" in order to describe a culture. Grounded theorists tend to rely on interviewing by way of eliciting participants' individual perspectives of a given social phenomenon. Ethnographies provide the reader with in-depth portrayals of social phenomenon, while grounded theorists facilitate the emergence of substantive theory that will, in turn, enlighten the research problematic, by having "immersed themselves" within the research context. Ultimately, both naturalistic forms of inquiry attempt to explain how people "understand their worlds."

The data was collected over a period of thirteen years, beginning in the mid 1990s to 2003, and is enriched with my practical work experiences with homeless youth populations. Structured and unstructured interviews were conducted with 180 street youth (44 in Toronto; 35 in Montreal; 70 in

Halifax, and 31 in Guatemala City), and with 49 service providers (18 in Toronto; 7 in Montreal; and 24 in Guatemala City). I also conducted participant and nonparticipant observations of street life and shelter culture in all four cities; and ten case studies of street youth shelters and programs (3 in Toronto; 1 in Montreal; 2 in Halifax; and 5 in Guatemala City). The interview questions were designed to tap into a range of the participants' experiences, from their lives prior to street life, on the streets, and for some, while exiting street culture. I was interested in how these young people perceived themselves throughout their street-life careers and how they made sense of their activities. My analyses involved open, axial, and selective coding techniques which fractured the data into conceptually-specific themes and categories; rebuilt the data in new ways by linking primary categories and auxiliary themes into a path analysis; and constructed a theoretical narrative shaped by data integration and category construction (Strauss and Corbin, 1990).

The following are brief descriptions of the study-case sites. Montreal's *Dans La Rue* (DLR), notably popular with hard-core street youth, is an alternative downtown street youth shelter and drop-in service. Toronto's *Covenant House* (CH) is a premier street youth service that offers short-term shelter, drop-in support, health and educational services, job training, and long-term housing. CH is the largest and best funded street youth agency in North America. *Casa Alianza* (CA) is an extensive network of street children services in Guatemala providing short and medium-term shelter, legal and health services, and detoxification locations. CA has been a leading advocate against the horrific abuse, torture, and death of street children by para-military forces throughout Guatemala. *The Center for Integral Community Development* (CEDIC) is a rural Guatemalan prevention program directed towards impoverished families and street workers (i.e., "ninos en la calle" or youth in the street), specializing in various community programs. *Street Kids International* (SKI) is a Toronto-based street youth advocacy program that has initiated community economic development programs throughout Africa and Asia. *Phoenix Youth Services* is a Halifax-based multipurpose youth center which houses a shelter, a drop-in center, education programs, and second stage housing. Finally, *ARK* is a small downtown Halifax drop-in center providing street youth with a supportive community space, food, clothing, showers, counseling and various skills training programs.

Why this book?

A study of street youth culture is important because the number of young people living on the streets continues to increase each year. Despite this astonishing reality, not much is known about the actual experiences of street youth and their engagement with the different stages of street life. Moreover, definitive information on the types of organizations that exist to help this population is limited. While there are a number of academic studies of homeless youth, there is little in the way of analyses that take into account the first-hand experiences of those youth actually living on the street. As a result, there is a dearth of information on what constitutes best practices with the various populations of homeless youth.

My aim in this book is to impart portraits of young people on the street that are hopefully more comprehensive than existing studies. By focusing on the stories related by street youth themselves as they discover their individual voices, my aim is to contribute to a detailed understanding of how young people end up on the street, what happens to them on the street, and how some manage to leave street culture. Readers will encounter personal perspectives of both street life and human service organizations as they are experienced by street youth.

Presently, we in North and Latin America are in the midst of a social welfare system that is being dismantled. Services everywhere are having greater difficulty helping people who find themselves without work, without shelter, without food, without clothing, without personal supports, and/or without community. A pressing question is what happens to such vulnerable people. And what happens to their children for whom many become too powerless to care for. It is not only timely but imperative for societies to investigate the ramifications of increasingly individualist environments, and to understand the needs of those who are assuming progressively more the role of caring for society's disadvantaged. Youth shelters and services currently play a principal role in the lives of disadvantaged youth—as such, operating as "street level bureaucrats" (Lipsky, 1980) in scripting day-to-day public policy. It is my hope that this study will better serve social service providers and policy makers by illuminating the social worlds of street youth, as well as the critical roles played by volunteer agencies such as Toronto's Covenant House, Montreal's Dans La Rue, and Guatemala's Caza Alianza, as vital sources of aid and hope for children in need.

This introductory chapter provides an overview of the taxonomies used in academic studies and discussion of youth homelessness, a description of the methods employed in collecting and analyzing the research findings, and the rationale underlining aims of this book. Chapter Two highlights the various ways homeless youth have been understood and "treated" historically in North America and Europe within the context of general adult homelessness. Chapter Three poses the critical question how youth become homeless. I explore the various etiological analyses of homeless youth and investigate further the processes of youth engagement with street culture. Chapter Four presents a more detailed analysis of street culture and the various activities in which youth engage on the streets. More specifically, I attempt a mapping of the daily activities and interactions of homeless youth, highlighting the ways in which youth make sense of their homeless identities. In this chapter notions of street "acculturation" and "disengagement" are also explored as central concepts in understanding homelessness. Chapter Five focuses on organizational responses by analyzing the "types" of human service organizations working with these populations, as well as how homeless youth interact with various organizations. A theoretical discussion of organizational responses is documented along with "lessons from the field" concerning best practices in attracting and working with street youth populations. Chapter Six concludes this study with a summation of significant findings and aims to provide realistic commentaries for best practice.

A History of Homelessness in Western Society: From the Spiritual Wanderer to the Squeegee Kid

Homelessness is not a new phenomenon. Throughout history, the image of homelessness has been variously portrayed, usually reflecting the values of the dominant culture of the historical period in which they are in use. In Ancient Greece, for example, the beggar was regarded as the lowest of lowly creatures (even more than a slave) because of his or her lack of attachment and belonging. In contrast, the idea of "holy poverty," prevalent previous to the sixteenth century, stemmed from the Christian Church's belief in the spiritual wanderer void of worldly possessions, as a worthy being. Yet in the middle ages, the beggar was considered suspect and dangerous, leading possibly to open brigandage. The "hoboes" and "tramps," in more recent times, formed a majority in the vast armies of itinerant workers during the Great Depression of the early to mid-twentieth century. The last several decades have witnessed the emergence of skid rows and the so called "bums" or "skid-rowers" who continue to inhabit those districts (Baum and Burns, 1993; Hoch, 1987; Hopper, 1990; Katz, 1986). As Hopper (1990:320) notes, "if not the person, then at least the image of homelessness has undergone significant rehabilitation."

During the 1980s throughout North America homelessness re-emerged; this time defined as a significant social problem. As noted by Baum and Burnes (1993:1) at the beginning of their analysis of homelessness in the United States: "In the early 1980s, America became aware of the homeless."

This recognition continues today as it is possible to open up any daily newspaper that covers a North American city, and likely there will be at least one article discussing one aspect or another of the plight of our homeless.

> For more than a decade, the American public has been bombarded by images of homeless men, women, and children roaming the streets and sleeping in cardboard boxes or in doorways. (Baum and Burnes, 1993:86)

While homelessness has worn assorted masks at different times, it has been a steady facet of North American culture with a very long history.

An overwhelming sense of alienation, isolation, and suffering bind all who have been and who continue to be homeless across time and geography. The following excerpt lists the range of misery, misfortune, and circumstances that characterized the lives of those who constituted the homeless in eighteenth-century France:

> Widows, orphans, cripples . . . journeymen who had broken their contracts, out of work laborers, homeless priests with no living, old men, fire victims . . . war victims, deserters, discharged soldiers and even officers . . . would be vendors of useless articles, vagrant preachers with or without licenses, "pregnant servant-girls and unmarried mothers driven from home," children sent out "to find bread or maraud. . . ." (Hopper, 1990:309)

Hopper's (1990:311) conviction that "homelessness has traditionally been viewed as a problem of troubled and troublesome individuals" remains nonetheless accurate today.

Significantly, in so far as homelessness is not a recent phenomenon, its increased visibility in contemporary Middle America is.[1] As Jencks (1994: v) explains:

> Late in the 1970s Americans began noticing more people sleeping in public places, wandering the streets with their possessions in shopping bags, rooting through garbage bins in search of food or cans, and asking for handouts. . . .

The last three decades witnessed both more homeless individuals and the development of a large number of different services, such as soup kitchens, drop-in centers, and shelters in the majority of North American cities (Baum and Burnes, 1993; Hetzberg, 1992; Hopper, 1990; Price, 1989; Stark, 1994). In fact, Jencks (1994:103) notes, that "by the late 1980s America had created a network of shelters and soup kitchens that serviced between 200,000 and 300,000 people a day."[2]

Historical responses to homelessness

The truth is homelessness is not new, nor are our efforts to respond to it
substantially different from those of our forebears.
Baum and Burnes, 1993:91

Throughout history, responses to homelessness were frequently shaped by processes of criminalization, in which a homeless person was perceived and treated as a social "deviant." Enforced imprisonment, compulsory work, banishment, branding, pillory, and torture (Hopper, 1990), were some of the punitive practices used to manage and control the homeless in a variety of classified settings designed to further contain these populations, such as poorhouses, police stations, and municipal lodging houses[3] (Baum and Burnes, 1993; Platt, 1969).

As early as the Ancient Greeks, the delivery of welfare relief was dependent upon deciding who was "deserving" and who was "undeserving."[4] As such, the idea of welfare relief has long been associated with ideas of work and labor as a means of guarding against "providing something for nothing." Policy makers and practitioners alike have consistently been concerned with charity being too generous and promoting dependency. This fear, consequently, led to the development of the notion of scientific charity, which in turn formed part of the historical framework for that which is known today as professional social work. The first civil and secular statement concerning poverty, contained in the Poor Laws, regarded almsgiving as a cause of poverty and emphasized controlled relief and labor (Henry, 1987). Contemporary critics like Hopper (1990:312), however, have argued that the conventional notion of poor relief and of emergency shelters (in the form of settlement houses, police jails, and almshouses) were tied to the notion of "less eligibility"—of making a situation less attractive as a means of weeding-out those who "really needed" assistance from those who may simply have wanted a "free ride." Hopper's argument illustrates how traditional welfare relief is anchored in the discriminatory categories of deserving and undeserving; of, in other words, the good and the bad. In order to be given a bed, one was required to "show need" in the form of, for example, submitting to intrusive and personal questioning, being willing to perform work and house chores, or attending a religious sermon. Many authors have noted that given the conditions of public housing in the late nineteenth century which have been variously described as "spartan," "unforgiving," "disgusting," and "cruel," the mere fact that one was requesting a bed was proof enough of desperation and need (Hopper, 1990). An 1857 report by commissioners of the poor, describes a South Carolina poorhouse as follows:

> The yard was uncleansed—the surface drain filled with offensive matter—the Privies in a most filthy state—the floors most unwashed, many of the windows obscured by apparently many months accumulation of dust and cobwebs—nearly all the beds and bedding in a disgustingly neglected state, and in some localities, swarming with vermin. (Katz, 1986:26)

From years spent in the field and in reviewing of the literature, Baum and Burnes (1993) contend little has changed within the American welfare reform movement, beginning with the nineteenth-century poorhouse to the early twentieth-century municipal lodges, and continuing straight through to our present-day shelter system. Others such as Lipton, Sabatini, and Micheals (1986:38) argue we have come full circle and that "we [now] have the most poorly organized system of care since we started with the almshouses in 1750." Generally, societies of the past and present have consistently vacillated between a desire to reform or, alternatively, to punish the pauper seeking relief. An excerpt from a 1934 study of the homeless in New York recounts:

> Dependent homeless persons have always been a problem in New York City and, whether by discipline or charity, or both, the attention of the public has been challenged on numerous occasions. . . . (Hopper, 1990:310)

Even the Christian Church recanted its earlier view of "poverty as sacred," replacing it with the notion of "sloth as sin," and sanctified industry and work.

When the tides of mendicancy continued to grow throughout the fifteenth century, so did the public's fear, disillusionment, and indignation. The growth in the number of poor gradually became seen as commonplace, part and parcel of everyday life. By the sixteenth century, "the conjuncture of older problems with poverty, with population growth and economic expansion" spurred the "international movement for welfare reform on the European continent" (Hopper, 1990:305). A new welfare system was needed when the medieval institution of charity proved inadequate in dealing with the many changes wrought by increased industrialization and by the spread of capitalism, which in turn had generated a notable trend in rural-to-urban migration. City parishes failed to manage the growing numbers of dislocated peasantry. By the mid-nineteenth century, the United States, fresh from the Civil War, amassed a new homeless population made up of widows, orphans, war veterans, and freed slaves, who joined the ranks of those already homeless immigrants, urban poor, and other victims of urbanization and industrialization (Baum and Burnes, 1993). The ambulatory and derelict existence of those "wretched masses" prompted the emergence of a need for a better classification system for identifying those who really needed relief from those who, it was thought, were merely vagabonds or beggars, and as a result lazy and therefore undeserving of social assistance.

By the turn of the twentieth century, responsibility for the care of the poor shifted away from the medieval church in Europe to the family and the community, as well as to the almshouses and workhouses in the American colonies and, finally, to the beginning of a centralized secular welfare institution. Within this newfangled system, inexperienced and/or imprudent practitioners perceived the undeserving as a great threat. This perception was due in part to the public's fear of the beggar or drifter that was fueled by the widespread belief typifying the beggar as a thief or robber. More importantly, the "undeserving" constituted an even greater threat to public welfare in the eyes of social workers and policy makers because of the growing importance of the factory in the social and political economy of the new world. Industrialization and urbanization required a disciplined and diligent labor force. Highlighted in an 1834 manuscript is the fine line dividing the "deserving" and the "undeserving" within an overarching explanation of how poverty results from "our misfortunes," while pauperism materializes out of one's bad habits and indolence. From this simplistic conceptual framework, clearly lacking in consideration of the inequitable conditions that inform our everyday lives (then and now), followed the notion that "relief to the poor was charity; relief to paupers increased 'the evil in a tenfold degree'" (Katz, 1986:19).

Hoboes were tolerated within colonial North America insofar as they were not feared nor hated as much, primarily because they worked (albeit in a transient fashion) and were not dependent upon public assistance. Conversely, the tramp was mistrusted and the object of social animosity precisely because of his/her dependence on public welfare and presumed disdain for work (Baum and Burnes, 1993). Katz (1986:92) relates the traditional perception of tramps as "lazy, dishonest agitators living off the sentimental generosity of soft hearted women and the public bounty of poorhouses." Thus, the emergence at this time of a rational poor relief system quite consciously intended to discriminate among the poor—to discourage neediness and laziness while upholding the righteousness of work and wage. Jencks (1994:118) attempts to explain why homelessness has been framed within this particular dichotomy:

> But most of us do feel an obligation to help people who either cannot help themselves or are trying to do so and simply need an opportunity. Most Americans also know that some of the homeless fit this description, though they have no idea how large the proportion is. They badly want some way of distinguishing those who have a claim on society from those who do not. Offering everyone work is the most obvious test.

We can trace the continuation of this trend to the present day with the United States Congress in 1967 moving to get recipients "off the welfare rolls and onto payrolls" (Jencks, 1994:110). More recently, two 1993 poll-surveys (*Yankelovich and Associated Press*) found that a large majority of Americans favour work requirements for welfare recipients (including those with preschool children) (Jencks, 1994). Presently, the Canadian Government is rethinking its social assistance programs for single mothers due largely to a neoconservative attitude that implies ". . . she's [single mothers] the 90's version of the welfare bum, voluntarily choosing to reproduce outside wedlock and raising troubled kids in bad neighborhoods" (Speirs, 1998).

In the words of Baum and Burnes (1993:11), "for more than a decade, America has experienced a love-hate relationship with the homeless." Even though, on one hand, it can be argued that the love-half of that equation is understated, there has nevertheless existed a sentiment of pity, compassion and desire to help others in need (for a variety of reason). On the other hand, fear, indignation, and frustration have spurred the idea that "nothing can be done"; in effect, the belief that we are helpless to affect the lives of those around us, especially among them the undeserving. Extending this notion further, welfare history in general is rooted in two diametrically opposed paradigms—one informed by notions of justice, (in)equality, and difference, and the other by western capitalism and liberalism that are, in turn, informed by a strong Protestant work ethic.

Currently, homelessness has taken on the collective image of single parents, abused children, and whole families[5] that have been hit by family dysfunction (specifically in the case of runaway youth). Also contributing to this collective picture are external events that affect the organization or structure of our lives, such as, for example, the polarization of the labor market with highly paid skilled jobs on one end and low paid unskilled jobs on the other, and the scarcity of affordable housing.[6] Recent ethnographic and naturalistic accounts have refocused the image of "being homeless" through a different lens, altering its definition from its earlier more positivist renderings (see for example, the work of Ferrill, 1991; Liebow, 1993; Snow and Anderson, 1993). Homelessness today is often presented as episodic,[7] with many homeless maintaining ties with family and friends, some still working, and many still retaining some control over their lives. Mitch Snyder and other homeless advocates (especially from the Community for Creative Non-Violence in Washington, DC) are largely responsible for giving homeless people a political voice and for providing the public with a more compassionate picture of this population. Perhaps the recent sympathetic view of homelessness emanates from our own fears that it can happen to us. As Jencks thoughtfully explains,

> During the early 1980s, the economically vulnerable population grew while the odds that its members would become homeless remained relatively constant. During the late 1980s, the economically vulnerable population grew far less, but the odds that its members would become homeless rose. (1994:58)

A compassionate picture of homelessness may be further bolstered by the findings of recent qualitative investigations, which reveal in those who are without a home the characteristics of agency, resilience, and resourcefulness (Karabanow, 2003; Kozol, 1988; Wagner, 1993). Despite this data, the image of the homeless loner as a drunkard, as mentally ill, lazy, or dangerous nonetheless retains a powerful symbolism within our collective consciousness.[8]

Homeless youth in history

Organized responses to homeless youth have differed consistently in one fundamental way from those designed for homeless adults. This difference is based upon the premise that those in the helping profession generally believed the young person could be "reformed" or "transformed" into a conscientious citizen. The late nineteenth century (early Progressive era) represented a shift from social Darwinism and the belief that delinquent and dependent children were inherently evil, towards a belief in the importance of one's environment in shaping character and values. In other words, the prominent philosophical debate of nature versus nurture which sharply influenced popular thought throughout the mid-nineteenth century, had also permeated the realm of social work.

In the United States during the early nineteenth century bands of street children, known derogatively as "roving street Arabs," increasingly populated inner cities (for example, by 1860, New York reported more than 30,000 street youth)—the majority orphaned, castaways, abandoned, and/or runaways (Teeter, 1995). Much like today's street youth, they were involved in activities that were considered then and now legitimate (e.g., selling newspapers and food) and illegitimate (e.g., prostitution and drug dealing) street trades (Teeter, 1995).

Impoverished children, those on the streets, and/or having difficulties with families, were taken out of urban settings and placed in cottage-like reformatories situated in rural areas, in settings valued for their "naturalness." These reformatories, which sprang up throughout Western Europe and North America, were expected to "remedy the neglect and vice of parents, the failure of public schools, of missions and Sunday schools, and other moral agencies in the outside world" (Platt, 1969:52). Much like other forms of relief during this period, reformatories were laden with the philosophy and rhetoric of the Protestant work ethic. Initiated by the "child savers," a middle class, religious, and philanthropic women's movement, the reformatory transformed the child welfare system (consisting primarily of orphanages and almshouses) through teaching those "in care," the middle-class values distilled in the westernized notions of family, work, and religion (Platt, 1969; Teeter, 1995). Although street youth were sympathetically viewed as having been robbed of their childhood, their daily street activities were nonetheless understood to comprise a threat to urban development and, more generally, to the capitalist democratic order.[9] In theory, the reformatory was intended to provide "delinquent" and dependent youth with a gentler, more caring environment than the urban almshouse and local jail. In reality, however, reformatories became training institutions and industrial schools with the purpose of teaching youth lower-class working skills:

Industrial education, as it was euphemistically called, was derived from new developments in educational theory. The training of "delinquents" in manual and low-skilled jobs was justified as an educational enterprise because it was consistent with the rhetoric and aims of the child savers. (Platt, 1969:60–61)

The reformatory's doctrine of training the deviant, delinquent, or dependent child, as street children were variously called, stemmed from the principle that these individuals were "trainable," in the sense having the ability to change through obedience, rather than by learning. The child-savers movement cherished the belief that these wayward children, who were predominantly Black and of immigrant origin, could be reformed. While this notion still holds prominence today, the homeless adult is, in contrast, less often afforded such a position.

In the mid- to late nineteenth-century street youth continued to be seen as depraved, immoral, and evil. Consequently, new strategies were employed to "clean up" city streets. In the United States, the public school system was established to deal with vagrancy and delinquency. Public schooling was intended to import character-building to this "problematic" youth population, as well as moral and religious education (Nelson, 1995; Teeter, 1995). Similarly, during the 1860s, the Young Men's Christian Association emerged to provide healthy home-like structures for street youth within the urban setting. In addition, many cities adopted the Truancy Act to provide local authorities with the power to apprehend young people wandering the streets. Children's Aid Societies were also founded during this time as a mechanism to oversee the perceived growing delinquency and gang activity of street youth populations (Nelson, 1995). Aid Societies functioned as moral agents emblazoned with the mission of "washing away" the evils of crime, poverty, unemployment, and laziness perceived in street youth populations.

The stereotypes responsible for shaping Euro-American ideas of homeless youth, are similar to those that have informed our ideas of homelessness in general, in that they too have a history of image transformations. For instance, early nineteenth-century labeling referred to street youth as "petty thieves," "street sinners," "street urchins," and "begging impostors," while in the early twentieth century street youth were commonly branded as "young barbarians" and "street wandering children." By the 1950s, popular perceptions of this same population were influenced by notions of psychological deviance; street youth were thought to be mentally disturbed. Just twenty years later in the 1970s, we renamed street youth yet again, calling them this time "enfants perdus," which is to say, our lost children. The present day image of street youth is that of the sexually and/ or physically abused runaway.

The differing nomenclatures were paternalistic, reflecting western society's dominant philosophical tendency of the day. For instance, in 1869 when the evolutionary theories of Charles Darwin had captivated both scientific and popular thinking, ten years after the appearance of his *On the Origin of Species* (1859), an official of the Children's Aid Society compared homeless boys to roving animals:

> . . . Enjoying the idle and lazzaroni life on the docks living in the summer almost in the water, and curling down at night, as the animals do, in any corner they can find . . . this is without a doubt in the blood of most children—as an inheritance, perhaps from some remote barbarian ancestor—a passion for roving. (Rivlin and Manzo, 1988:27–28)

In contrast, Robertson (1992:288) describes the common psychiatric understanding of homeless youth that helped shape the image of this population in the 1950s and 1960s, during a period when psychoanalysis was at the forefront of accepted wisdom:

> Individuals characteristically escape from threatening situations by running away from home for a day or more without permission . . . typically they are immature and timid and often feel rejected at home, inadequate, friendless. They often steal furtively.

Ruddick's (1996) comprehensive analysis of homeless youth in Hollywood highlights a series of changes from the 1970s onward that were responsible for initiating a shift away from the image of the street youth as a juvenile delinquent and criminal. A more sympathetic image of homeless youth resulted from a number of key factors. The deinstitutionalization of the runaway from the juvenile penal system, combined with an increase in public recognition of the reality of abuse within dysfunctional families,[10] along with the lack of employment and shelter opportunities for this population all played central roles in the transformation of the popular perception of street youth. A crucial outcome of those changes was the novel awareness that these children had been forgotten or had "slipped through the cracks" of the conventional child welfare system.

The street youth of today evokes varied images that include young mothers, runaways, immigrant youth, and "squeegee kids." A single though significant element binding these perceptions together is the growing acceptance that street youth exist because of reasons beyond their own control. A recent study of street youth in Halifax, Nova Scotia, found that over 60% of public citizens interviewed perceived the root causes of youth homelessness as other than individual pathology (Karabanow, 2004B). Today's young person on the street is often thought to be fleeing an abusive, dysfunctional family life or a miserable institutional situation, who finds refuge on the street or in a short-term emergency shelter. In the contemporary social work schema, fault is redirected away from the individual and placed upon such sociopolitical factors as housing, employment, and family and/or institutional inadequacy.

Who are the present-day homeless?

Just as in the past, the many faces of homelessness today continue to generate academic debates about the language used to characterize this population. As noted by Lipton and Sabitini (1984:156):

> The term "homeless" is actually a catchword that focuses our attention on only one aspect of the individual's plight: his [sic] [and her] lack of residence or housing. In reality, the homeless often have no job, no function, no role within the community; they generally have few if any social supports. They are jobless, penniless, functionless, and supportless as well as homeless.

Conversely, in their study of New England homeless youth, Vissing and Diament (1995), argue that a more accurate term to describe this phenomenon would be "housing distress." As such, who the homeless are seems to depend on where one is looking. Major metropolises in the Eastern Coast of the United States, for instance, have a high number of African-Americans, while the West Coast hosts a high number of Hispanics. It matters equally who is doing the looking, as some authors argue that the homeless population consists largely of drug addicts and mental patients, while others tend to describe out-of-work families as the main contributors to homelessness. Despite these limiting viewpoints, most writers generally agree that the homeless population is heterogeneous, comprising battered and abandoned women, single mothers, evicted families, single unemployed and older women, deinstitutionalized mental patients, illegal immigrants, street youth, drug addicts, alcoholics, and those living on skid row.

Confusion also exists regarding how many people are homeless—the estimates have varied from official American government estimates (HUD) of 250,000, to those of homeless advocates who see the population approximating an excess of 3 million in the United States alone. Moreover, researchers involved in counting this population utilize diverse methods of tabulation such as counting the number of individuals, the number of homeless household units, or using a random night count of all shelters, of streets, parks, and local hang outs, thus resulting in very little unanimity of vision.

One problem faced by researchers in counting homeless youth is that adolescents are frequently shrouded by invisibility. By staying in places where they will not be identified, or by living with friends and sleeping in squats, street youth create a "hidden culture."[11] Despite this obstacle the numbers of street youth already reported have been alarming: 30,000 in Montreal; 35,000 in Toronto; 200,000 in Mexico City; over 2 million in the United States; and approximately 30 million in Brazil. While these numbers are indeed shockingly high, they are relative to the overall population of the cities in question. Moreover, Carrizosa and Poertner (1992:405) aptly note in their study of Latin American street children, "as with most social problems, it is difficult to get accurate estimates, and part of this difficulty lies in the problem of definition."

Adult homelessness

Until recently, the majority of research on adult homelessness has been in the form of surveys designed to focus upon, what Snow and Anderson (1993:18) contend to be the "demographics and disabilities of the homeless." These studies have provided useful information for those involved in policy development, yet have told us little about one's life as homeless—its nature and texture. As such, this body of literature has constructed what social scientists have termed "experience distant" as opposed to "experience near" knowledge of study subjects (Geertz, 1983). Consequently, there has been a recent "sprinkling" of ethnographies (Kozol, 1988; Liebow, 1993; Snow and Anderson, 1993) that have explored what it means to be homeless from the point of view of the homeless person. The most strident debate within the literature is whether adult homelessness is more a function of individual pathologies or of structural inefficiencies.[12]

Supporters of the structural camp in this particular debate, such as prominent U.S. scholars Blau (1992), Rossi (1989), and Wright (1989), have vociferously contended that homelessness on the whole is fundamentally a problem of housing, the solution to which is the creation of adequate low-income housing. Jencks (1994), also an affiliate of the structural camp, summarizes the major factors put forth to explain the current homeless rash in the United States: elimination of involuntary commitment; the eviction of mental hospital patients who have no place to go; increases in long term joblessness; and political restrictions on the creation of flop-houses.

Kozol's widely read report on poverty, *Rachel and Her Children* (1988), supports Jencks' contention that homelessness is a symptom of structural factors:

> Unreflective answers might retreat to explanations with which readers are familiar: "family breakdown," "drugs," "culture of poverty," "teen pregnancies," "the underclass," etc. While these are precipitating factors for some people, they are not the cause of homelessness. The cause of homelessness is the lack of housing. (12)

Conversely, Baum and Burnes (1993) defend the individual pathologies paradigm as a result of their experiences working in an American church-based homeless organization. They argue that a focus upon structural causes (loss of housing, jobs, and security net), and consequently, structural solutions (policies that ensure adequate housing and full employment, and restore social welfare programs), ignores what they believe are the "real" issues causing homelessness. According to Baum and Burnes, homelessness is directly related to mental illness, drug and alcohol addictions, lack of education and skills, and low self esteem. "We would like to believe that homeless people are 'just like us, but have had a really bad break,' but it isn't true" (Baum and Burnes, 1993:15–16). Further, after reviewing some of the literature on homelessness, Baum and Burnes (1993:29) conclude that somewhere between 65 and 85 percent of the homeless population in the United States suffer from one or a combination of the above mentioned personal pathologies. While the writers do acknowledge the factors articulated by Jencks (1994),[13] they note: ". . . what we saw instead were people frustrated and angered by personal lives out of control"[14] (Baum and Burnes, 1993:2). Essentially, Baum and Burnes contend that by ignoring the individual dimensions which they argue contribute to homelessness, and by primarily focusing on the structural and social elements, "America is in deep denial" (Baum and Burnes, 1993:3).

Being poor, however, does not equate to homelessness. To be sure, some economically underprivileged people maintain ties with and seek support within their families, friends, and communities. In contrast, homeless people, argue Baum and Burnes, do not have any of what Wiseman (1970) refers to as social margin or social support networks.[15] As stated by Bahr (1990:xxi): "Homelessness . . . is a condition of disaffiliation, a lack of bonds, a pathology of connectedness, and not an absence of proper housing." To deny the "real" causes of homelessness, Baum and Burnes conclude, will only create ineffective services and powerlessness within the population:

> . . . [Shelter] facilities that do nothing more than warehouse people who are seriously impaired and where there is little attempt to provide the help they so desperately need . . . Instead of confronting the troubling realities of addictions and mental illness, our society has doubly victimized the homeless by its obstinate denial. (Baum and Burnes, 1993:74)

The manner in which we support the homeless through housing options has amplified the aforementioned debate.

Adult shelters

> A large room off the lobby is filled with over 100 men. Some lie curled up on the dirty floor; a few are in various stages of undress; others gesture wildly in the air talking to themselves. Some just sit staring into space. The stench of urine and unwashed bodies is strong. (excerpt from Nancy Rhoden, quoted in Baum and Burnes, 1993:75)

In North American cities during the 1980s the official solution to homelessness was to ensure homeless people were fed and sheltered. As such, the private and public shelter emerged as the response to homelessness, leading many authors to characterize the 1980s as the decade of "shelterization" (Barak, 1991; Baum and Burnes, 1993; Hoch and Slayton, 1989; Ruddick, 1996; Tiernan, Horn, and Albelda, 1992; Timmer, 1988).[16] While shelters, as we have seen, are not new and have a long history, they have become predominant in the late twentieth century primarily because the traditional institutions of the family and the parish are no longer held responsible for dependent people, and because our welfare state has been shown to respond inadequately with its rigid welfare laws.

Research on "shelter culture" has focused primarily upon public shelters for adults in the United States. Those investigations have repeatedly highlighted the degrading characteristics of shelter life, providing vivid descriptions of the physical environments that are often seen and experienced as filthy, violent, and dehumanizing (Baum and Burnes, 1993; Baxter and Hopper, 1981; Hopper, 1990; Rossi, 1989), and which are organized according to a myriad of oppressive rules and regulations (Liebow, 1993; Stark, 1994; Timmer, 1988).[17] Other observers have noted the manner by which shelters legitimize and perpetuate social marginality (Hoch, 1987), and at the same time, the status quo, thereby guaranteeing shelter workers' jobs, and in a greater sense, the shelter industry (Barak, 1991; Baum and Burnes, 1993; Tiernan, Horn and Albelda, 1992). In reality, some have argued, many shelters are administrative "shambles" (Hopper, 1990), allowing such practices as "creaming" the best clients (through stringent entrance requirements) (Baum and Burnes, 1993; Morse, 1992; Weinreb and Rossi, 1995). Still some argue shelters produce a dependent and non-motivated or institutionalized population (Baum and Burnes, 1993; Cuomo, 1992; Drake, Osher and Wallach, 1991), and create an environment of social control that approaches sociologist Erving Goffman's (1961) notion of the "total institution" (Gounis, 1992; Keigher, 1992; Snow and Anderson, 1993; Stark, 1994; Timmer, 1988). Some conservatives have cynically argued that shelters provide residents with more dispensable income for drugs and alcohol because they render services free of charge.[18]

Rossi's (1989:103) homeless survey in New York City during the early 1980s revealed that jails were preferred over shelters because they were experienced as safer, cleaner places, providing greater privacy and serving a higher quality of food. In her case study of a shelter for homelesss adults, Jewell (1993) argues that shelters have failed in part because they are seen as "storage bins" and lack a comprehensive understanding of homelessness that would address more than just the issue of housing. Hopper (1990: 317) suggests that the modern-day shelter is simply the almshouse in disguise and functions as a "dumping ground for the misfits and discards of other public facilities." Similarly, Scull (1977:33) sees the shelter as "a convenient way of getting rid of inconvenient people."

In summary, there is little that is positive to say about our present-day public shelter system. According to most researchers in Western Europe and in North America, shelters have failed in terms of providing refuge and rehabilitation. This failure, it has been argued, is in part to our collective indecisiveness about whether this population merits "true help." Since the question of who is to blame for this phenomenon continues to be debated, we have yet to decide on whether the homeless adult falls into the "deserving" or "undeserving" camp. Our solutions, therefore, are, at best, poor band-aid responses. The only bright light has come from discussions concerning voluntary adult/youth shelters. With the appearance in the 1970s of new types of homeless people—women with children, youth and young families—the voluntary shelter re-emerged to provide emergency shelter, food, and clothing in a drastically different way than the traditional welfare system. This form of provision has been seen by some as a return to "classical charity" (Henry, 1987) and will be the focus of Chapter Five. The following two chapters focus specifically on youth homelessness.

CHAPTER THREE

Where Do They Come From?
The Etiology of Street Youth

*The problem of homeless and runaway youths . . . continues to escalate. Young
people run away or find themselves homeless for a variety of reasons, including
family contact and/or sexual abuse, family breakup due to homelessness,
aging out of foster care, struggles with sexual orientation issues, substance
abuse, serious health problems (i.e., HIV/AIDS), school truancy or dropout,
and poverty-related situations. The streets—with their myriad dangers—are
usually the first refuge for these youths.*
The Child Welfare League of America, 1991:3

Why kids run

Most of the research on street youth has been etiological; that is, concerned with the assignment of causes. Popular and academic interest has
focused on finding reasons for why homeless young people exist in North
and South/Latin America and, in particular, why homelessness continues
to grow. The bulk of representative writings on street youth, primarily
concerned with etiology as it were, can be divided along two separate lines
of reasoning with respect to the role of running away in the lives of the
street youth.

Before 1980, street youth were essentially understood by way of their
personal pathologies, and much attention was placed upon individual factors, like the need for independence, the refusal to abide by rules, the quest
for fun and excitement, involvement with drugs and alcohol, and the desire for sexual freedom. It was commonly accepted by researchers and welfare workers that life on the streets was a matter of individual choice.

These early accounts focused primarily on finding the causes of running in the individual. It was believed that runaways suffered from "substantially more personality pathologies" including one researcher's notion of a "runaway reaction disorder" (Jenkins, 1971:169). Poor self esteem, immature and withdrawn personalities, depressive and anti-social character structure (Stierlin, 1973), were all understood as characteristic of the "depressed-withdrawn, uncommunicative and delinquent" profiles associated with "psychopaths and patterns of maladjustment" (Edelbrock 1980:218–22).

Some studies identified family pathologies as another key difference between runaways and non-runaways. With that in mind, it has thus been contended that "running away . . . is the surface manifestation of deep psychosocial conditions" located in primary family relations (Stierlin 1973: 61). It was also thought that runaways ultimately perceived their parents as "significantly less supportive and more punishing" than the parents of non-runaways (Brandon 1974), and are more likely to come from broken homes characterized by poor parent-child relations (D'Angelo, 1974; Adams, Gullotta and Clancy, 1985). Several studies also note that runaways report parental physical and/or sexual abuse as a major reason for running (Farber and Kinast 1984, Janus et al 1987, Kufeldt and Nimmo 1987, Price 1989, and Weber 1991). Troubles at school, as well as a variety of less consistent factors, have also been identified as distinguishing runaways from non-runaways. Runaways are more likely to report poor grades, trouble with teachers, disinterest in school and a general inability to relate to adults (Goldmier and Dean 1972), limited educational goals (D'Angelo 1974), and more behavioral as well as academic problems in school (Olson, Liebow, Mannino, and Shore, 1980).

In contrast to this distressing psychosocial portrait of street youth and their backgrounds, there have been several efforts to present "running" as a normal extension of adolescent desires for freedom, independence, adventure, and for pleasure away from the "adult world" (Yablonsky, 1968). This perspective, however, was formulated prior to the "discovery" of child abuse, and has since been largely rejected as "naive and inaccurate" (McCarthy 1990:24). Stating the obvious, one girl in Jack Rothman's (1991:1) study of runaway and homeless youth asks "why would any kid leave a happy environment?"

The last two decades have witnessed a greater understanding of the structural elements which place youth at risk. With the issues of despair,

systemic poverty, abuse, and alienation now at the forefront, a new perception of homelessness has surfaced; characterized as "running away from
something" rather than "running toward the streets." For the most part,
academic and professional literature now focuses on the circumstances
that lead youth to street life. Data that I collected from service providers
interviewed in Toronto, Montreal, and Guatemala City, reveals three substantial factors pushing adolescents to street life—internal family dysfunction, physical, sexual and/or emotional abuse, and poverty (Karabanow,
2003). While the debates that pit the concept of individual pathology
against that of environmental pressures remain ongoing, there exists far
more dialogue about youth "running away" or "escaping" from problematic situations, or about youth being "kicked out" or "thrown out" from
home, with the streets serving as a temporary safe haven. For instance, a
Toronto street youth who was interviewed exclaimed: ". . . don't you think
I'd go back home if I could, why would someone want to be out here on the
streets?" (Kandie, 17). In the following section I explore stories by street
youth with the aim of uncovering some of the reasons/causes why, for
these youth, living on the streets became a reality.

Etiological factors

While street youth populations are by no means homogeneous, they nonetheless present service providers with a number of shared experiences. A
prominent factor shaping the individual stories of the street kids from my
sample appears to be familial abuse, including sexual, emotional, and physical. The majority of participants in all of the four locations investigated for
this study, highlighted abusive family experiences, with street girls more
often describing sexual abuse by a male family member (usually a stepfather or mother's boyfriend) and street boys noting physical abuse by both
male and female family members. Both genders agreed that for the most
part, family life was characterized by violence, mistrust, and fear, with very
little evidence of feeling loved, cared for, and supported (emotional abuse):

> . . . There was a lot of arguing and fights at home with my mom. That's why I
> moved out. It wasn't working out. (Steve, 21, Halifax)

> When I hear youth talking about yeah I moved out because there were a lot of
> drugs, alcohol, I look at them and I'm like "I totally have respect for you be-

cause you made the move to get out of it." I've been through it and it's hard. When you're growing up as a kid and you're around all that stuff, it's really hard to go tell somebody, so you just end up living your life through it. It's really hard to live through . . . and then when you're a teenager and you can't take it anymore you try and get out . . . (Dola, 17, Guatemala)

Youth also commented that their "differences," such as their homosexuality and/or alternative lifestyles, marked major strains within family relations. Most often, one or both parents could not accept the youth's sexual orientation, leading to confrontation, alienation, and sometimes violence. Not surprising, the street can be perceived as a more accepting and sympathetic setting for youth who see themselves or are aware of being perceived as "different" or "not normal."

A majority of the participants in my research also described being "kicked out" or "pushed out" by parents or guardians. Reasons for such activity were commonly defined through family dysfunction, and as "tough love" approaches in dealing with problematic behaviors, and poverty. Over 85% of participants described family breakdowns (divorce, separation, or spousal abuse) and problematic relations with stepfathers/stepmothers: "My parents both split up and I ended up on the streets" (Abe, 18, Toronto); ". . . My parents got divorced when I was real young . . . my stepfather, we hate each other equally . . . when I was eleven I was in a group home . . . I was always in group homes . . . So I ran away at twelve . . . started to pull tricks [prostitute] with really ugly old men . . ." (Louise, 22, Halifax).

While several youth noted their involvement with drug use (especially heroin and cocaine) as the impetus for reaching the street, it was commonly contextualized within settings where parents and/or siblings were actively engaged in drug use/abuse/selling or settings characterized by extreme violence and poverty:

> I grew up in a really, really rough neighborhood . . . it's the five buildings that you can basically call a crack lot. There was a lot of drugs, a lot of alcohol, a lot of violence. . . . (Chris, 18, Montreal)

Significantly, many youth spoke about their feelings of not being loved, respected, or encouraged within the family unit. Nicko, for example, a nineteen-year-old Haligonian sadly remarked:

> She [mom] has told me this before; she has no faith in me. She thinks I'm going to be crawling back to her front door asking her to take me back. She

thinks I'm worthless. She has never given any motivation, she has never taken anything that's happened to me seriously, and she's more or less a person who has kids, but doesn't really care for them.

Interestingly and perhaps surprising too, many youth also described situations where their own behaviors were so problematic that it left little option for caregivers. It was further related that in those situations, many parents subscribed to a "tough love" approach—attempting to close off communication and/or contact with their child—a difficult task for both parent and child:

> Well I used to smoke a lot of dope and I just lost it and I was addicted to it and me and my mother were always arguing so she booted me out . . . she was kind of upset about it . . . and I was on the streets for three months. I was lonely, I was depressed, I felt like I didn't feel like being in this world and I always wanted to smoke dope and drink . . . I guess I had to learn the hard way. (Stan, 18, Montreal)

Stan later returned to his mother's house under the agreement to follow her rules, return to school and to stop his involvement with drugs and alcohol: ". . . My mother said 'if you skip any classes, if you're living here, I'm booting you out, you're out for good, I don't want nothing to do with you . . .' And I started to see that I was going to lose my mother, my own flesh and blood . . ." (Stan). Today Stan continues to live at home and will soon complete his high school education. For other youth, however, the tough love approach had generally resulted in more anger and confusion towards their families.

A more recent phenomenon in larger metropolises such as Toronto and Montreal is immigrant and refugee youth who have entered Canada illegally and/or without support. Those youth are predominantly from war-torn countries like Rwanda, Zaire, Congo, and Yugoslavia to name but a few. In Guatemala (as well as other developing countries in Central and South America), a growing population of street children are either orphans whose parents were killed in civil wars, by natural disasters or by disease, or displaced, again as a result of civil wars and natural disasters as well as extreme poverty. Moreover, in Guatemala and in Canada, increasing evidence points to a growing number of families which are predominantly matriarchal, and who are living in slums and shanty towns in Guatemala, and in North America, on sidewalks, in parks, and under bridges.

Related to this phenomenon are youth who work on the street in order to eke out a living for themselves and/or their families. Typical in North America are the "squeegee kids" who wait on busy urban street corners to wash the windshields of stopped cars. More common in Guatemala are the vociferous vendors, shoe shine boys, and flower sellers. In Guatemala, children provide an important source of additional income for impoverished families (Lave, 1995). Likewise, in his study of street children in Rio de Janeiro, Lusk confers that youth are working on "the street and earn money because there is not enough at home or because they have no alternative" (1992:296). Indeed, it has been suggested that street children in Latin America be primarily viewed as "workers," instead of as wayward or unfortunate youth (Lusk, Peralta and Vest 1989). The North American counterpart to the young street workers in Latin America could be the squeegee kid who has shown that this activity is primarily a form of income within an informal street-based economy. A markedly significant difference between squeegee kids in North American cities and youth street workers in Latin American cities is that the latter remains connected to mainstream institutions like the family and the school while the former demonstrates a discernible disassociation from mainstream culture.

Poverty is an overriding characteristic of all these populations in North, Central, and South America. The majority of street youth in underdeveloped and industrialized nations alike come from areas that are often the most affected by extreme poverty, such as rural regions, inner city ghettoes, and native reserves. Despite the existence of penury, Governments around the world become increasingly "laissez-faire" by increasing privatization and contracting, and by reducing spending on social assistance subsidies. By and large, many national governments repudiate direct action planning that would help to better the lives of their country's most vulnerable. Correspondingly, agencies that work with impoverished populations are increasingly underfunded and overutilized (see Karabanow, 2000). In this type of climate, it makes sense that the street has emerged as a "last resort" for increasing numbers of young people in crisis.

In this light, the street youth phenomenon can best be understood not as a problem of "social misfits" but as a problem of social structure. Time and time again, street youth populations report not only disturbing levels of poverty and neglect, but striking levels of abuse and dysfunction within the family, and overwhelming feelings of alienation and distance from mainstream culture as well. The following comment by a sixteen-year-old Toronto youth reveals the systemic ignorance and lack of support in his family and community:

> I used to live in a small rural community . . . they're very closed minded, ho-mophobic, racist people and when I was in high school and it was time for, I felt, to come out [announce one's homosexuality] the community along with my family were not very supportive . . . and my father kicked me out and I had nowhere to go . . . (Mike)

It is these precipitating factors, often interconnected, which "push" young people into street culture. While numerous studies have noted drug and al-cohol abuse, and the involvement in criminality and delinquency for a mi-nority of youth who still live in the home (prior to street embarkment), such activities are typically embedded within a dysfunctional social struc-tural context. The experience of one Guatemalan boy living on the street and with whom I spoke, attests to this point with a description of his skip-ping school and use of cocaine as coping strategies for physical abuse and poverty within the family. This scenario appears repeatedly in research studies on street youth as an organizing narrative in the lives of young peo-ple who eventually end up on the street.

With accounts of difficult family life for street youth populations now well documented, a surprisingly overwhelming link between child welfare experiences and street life has surfaced. The following section highlights some of these findings.

Street youth and the child welfare system

Over two thirds of the participants in my street youth research have had some form of experience with the child welfare system, such as involve-ment with group homes, foster care, residential facilities and case worker supervision. Street youth speak intensely about either "escaping" or "grad-uating" from such interactions. Common narratives of "escape" include frustrations with group homes and foster care settings, primarily concern-ing rules, staff, and other formal structures. Such frustrations are fre-quently exacerbated when many youth perceive themselves as victims of family abuse, but are treated as delinquents and/or criminals within the child welfare system. In Halifax, nineteen-year-old Trevor explains in an interview that "it was hard moving from one [foster] family to another family to another family . . . I have no kind of relation, nothing to them . . . it was hard." "Graduation" from the system (most commonly at the age of sixteen years) has been superceded for many adolescents with experiences of shelter and street living. The following remark by one Toronto youth shelter worker illustrates this point:

> I remember a staff member coming in all upset because she just got a call from a CAS [Children's Aid Society] worker who had said "I need a bed there [youth shelter] next week because this young person on my caseload is going to be sixteen next week and has to move out of the group home." I mean, how could CAS take someone into care, house them until sixteen and then boot them out?

Critical stances, such as this one above have been typically suppressed within the child welfare profession. In his analysis of the early child saver movement, Platt contends that:

> [M]uch of what passes as scholarly "research" tends to avoid issues that might be critical of responsible officials and management, and instead caters to facilitating the efficient and smooth operations of established systems. (1969:181)

Twenty years later, in his in-depth interviews with eight prostitutes, Edney (1988), argued that as an alternative to the family, social services have indeed failed, at least for several populations:

> The effectiveness of these agencies is not well documented but the evidence that is available suggests they are not particularly successful; it has been suggested that insensitive handling by social service agents may exacerbate the trauma suffered by the sexual abuse and incest victim. (28)

In fact, much of the literature regarding the child welfare system in North America points to the limitations of welfare systems in providing safe and compassionate environments for children. The small amount of information we know about formal child welfare institutions in Guatemala signals even worse scenarios of harsh treatment for children and youth, sparse living conditions, and a very correctional or rehabilitative philosophy of practice. As such, the literature reviewed here is critical, which is to say, it challenges the common perception of child welfare practice as being "for the best interest of the child."

Wilkinson (1987) discovered that the majority of her sample of Spokane street kids who had prior experience with foster care "found a lack of genuine care and concern for them on the part of foster parents" (75). Likewise, my own experiences with street youth reveals that a majority of institutionalized youth move from open to closed units, from foster care to group homes. This trajectory is informally known as making the "loop" within the system, and is a pattern which leaves youth feeling angry, confused, frustrated, and alone. A 1985 study by the Greater Boston Adolescent Emergency Service aptly describes the shelter hopping process within the child welfare system:

> As on a carousel, children . . . are placed on a painted pony which promises to take them to a safer world. For too many, however, their spinning wheel ride cycles them endlessly through the system with no planned destination. (Alleva, 1988:36–37)

The reality of Aleva's description of the "looping effect" of welfare services is exemplified in what this Haligonian street youth reported in my study:

> I was exactly sixteen years old, like I said I was in care for the majority of my young life and I was in five group homes, I was in three group homes and two foster families. And all but one of them, they were all physically and or sexually abusive. So I ended up being quite turned off to the whole in-care thing very quickly. So they day I turned 16 instead of going to my birthday party at the group home I used to live at and getting all my presents and supposedly be happy and what not, I woke up and said you guys get me the fuck out of here now, I don't care about the party, fuck the guests, fuck the cake, screw it I don't care. There's a shelter in Peterborough, take me there. (Tony, 22)

In a number of unpublished shelter reports Alleva finds 70% of sheltered youth had child welfare experience and, on average, sheltered youth have been found to move, "through six different living situations in a given year" (1988:36). In their study of 489 Calgary street kids, Kufeldt and Nimmo observe that 53% of the "runners" and 30% of the "in and outers" reported they were on the streets primarily because of earlier unconstructive encounters with child welfare agencies and, only secondarily, because of experiences with their biological parents. The authors conclude that the street has become a final resort once child welfare agencies "let them [street youth] down," leading to more neglect and abuse and "finally a sad, desperate death" (Kufeldt and Nimmo 1987:540).

A study of youth shelters in the southeastern United States by Kurtz, Jarvis and Kurtz (1991) found that homeless youth, compared to non-homeless youth, had extensive histories with child welfare agencies and "perceived the helping they received as punitive and harmful" (313). In addition, those youth had experienced so many placements within the youth care system that many "emotionally distance themselves from those who try to help in an attempt to protect themselves from the hurt of the separation they know to be inevitable" (313). Studies do, in fact, now suggest with greater regularity that street youth have run from child welfare institutions and agencies because of negative experiences. One notable study proposes that child welfare institutions produce street youth by inculcating learned helplessness—"an absence of any motivation to change a problematic situation" (van der Ploeg 1989:47). In a review of residential treatment of homeless youth, Morrissette and McIntyre (1989) underscore the isolation, anger, frustration, and inevitable failure incurred by the youth who have lived through a cycle of numerous placements, linear treatment strategies (i.e., fix the problem within the individual), and running away episodes. Their findings showed that, more often than not, homeless teenagers

> . . . described their negative experiences with social service agents as those where they were not heard or believed, where they were not considered capable of making decisions for themselves, and where they were dealt with punitively and in a controlling manner. (Michaud 1988:28)

The few reports from Guatemala also highlight the disturbing experiences of young people in institutional welfare settings. Documented are the stark physical environments, the unresponsive and often abusive staff, the strict rules and organization, and treatment typically reserved for criminals (Godoy, 1999; Human Rights Watch, 1997; Rizzini and Lusk, 1995).

Edney argues that "the very high rate of movement between placements suggests that the system, as it is currently set up, is not working for these juveniles" (1988:28). Welfare agents and agencies, he contends, can be divided between those which are punitive and controlling of juveniles and those which are described by welfare recipients themselves as helpful and supportive. When asked about negative experiences with social service agencies, Edney reports that his research participants "felt ignored, misunderstood, disbelieved and rejected. They also felt 'pushed around' because they were placed in venues without being consulted, and which they thought were untenable and inappropriate" (1988:68). Similarly, numerous authors can be cited for their documentation of the growing gap between the formal child welfare system and the available services for youth aged fourteen and up (Alleva, 1988; Karabanow, 2000; McCarthy, 1990). A sixteen-year-old Haligonian speaks to a consequence of this disparity:

> I'm not a priority for the CAS, my worker has a case load of probably 200 kids she's got to work and look after, I'm just not that big a priority . . . It's just basically what she keeps saying: "I'll do it [look for his identification] but you're not a priority anymore, you're out of care." (Terry, 16)

Although less common, positive experiences resulting from interactions between welfare providers and street youth, "where they [youths] were listened to, respected and understood," have been reported. "On these occasions they felt that they had some say in what would happen to them and some control over their lives" (Edney, 1988:68). Notably, those interactions were reported to be based on relationships of trust and acceptance and most frequently took place in alternative voluntary agencies (see Chapter Five).

Similarly, in his review of the child welfare system, Alleva (1988) notes that alternative youth service programs (such as drop-in centers and shelters) have a successful record of empowering youth. Empowerment has been achieved through the implementation of programs that require the participation of its youth clients at varying levels of planning, implementation, and overall operation of services themselves. Based on my own work experiences at Dans La Rue, a Montreal youth shelter and drop-in center, utilizing youth in the development and functioning of programs and services creates a sense of personal ownership, which enables youth to develop a sense of being in control of their lives, as well as being important to the lives of others within their communities. A principal outcome of this method of operation is greater self esteem for the youth involved (this will be explored in Chapter Five). Despite such constructive results, there is a clear lack of youth-centered services in the formal child welfare system:

> Self-help by urban youth are generally discredited and youth programs rarely involve young people in the decision making process. Rather than increasing opportunities for the exercise of legitimate power by adolescents, public agencies have opted for closer supervision as a means of decreasing opportunities for the exercise of illegitimate power. (Platt, 1969:180–81)

By way of bringing this chapter to a close, it is helpful to cite one of the few studies to focus on runaway youth, and the helping agencies aimed at that segment of the homeless population. Significantly, over one-half of those interviewed did not list any formal agency as being either helpful or appealing (Miller, Miller, Hoffman and Duggan, 1980:70). Moreover, one third said they felt more comfortable seeking help and advice from counterculture agencies such as free clinics, voluntary shelters, drop-ins centers, and crash pads, essentially because they were more "free," "unrestrained," "trustworthy," and met the basic needs of the youths requesting help. Over one-half of the interviewees suggested that an ideal agency would offer free food and shelter in a relaxed setting with sensitive staff who understood street life and who related to them on their own level. The authors of this enlightening study concluded that "our runaway subjects tended not to turn to formal agencies for help, but rather looked to counterculture or interpersonal networks for assistance" (73). Chapter Five will explore in greater detail the differences between formal and alternative street youth organizations. The following chapter looks at street youth culture and at the diverse activities in which street youth are involved.

CHAPTER FOUR

The Long and Winding Road:
La Rue, La Calle, and the Street

The recurrent debate about the origins and causes of homelessness that continues to shape discussions of homeless adults is considerably less focal in recent literature on homeless youth. In contrast to adults, homeless youth are generally perceived as a miscellaneous population running away from horribly abusive situations and surroundings. In upholding this view, the majority of authors have tended to pathologize the site of homelessness, which is to say, the street, as opposed to the homeless themselves.

A small number of studies have focused on street youth experiences of street life, emphasizing methods of survival, including in particular, one's reliance upon involvement in unconventional and criminal activities, such as drug use and sale, prostitution, panhandling, and theft. In two earlier surveys of transient youth at a Canadian hostel which were conducted by the Canadian Council on Social Development in 1970 and 1971, the most common sources of income while "living on the street" were identified as employment, contributions from friends, and panhandling. More recent studies, however, have underscored progressive involvement by youth in various forms of criminal activity as pivotal to their survival strategies on the street. The "process" of becoming a runaway is delineated in a 1984 study by Joseph Palenski. In his analysis, Palenski identifies the stages involved in the making of street "careers," as a sequence of related activities which contribute to the development of a typical "lifestyle" for runaways (90). This succession of events characteristically begins with the adolescent first leaving school. After failing to secure a job, the adolescent then begins to "hang-out" with friends who share survival information. Finally, the adolescent is said to be living on the street in a "runaway lifestyle" with the introduction of "hustling," defined as "a systematic procedure used to take something of value from others" which might include prostitution, the selling of drugs, purse snatching, and cheating individuals or agencies of money. Palenski's schema presents illegal behaviour as a response to the conditions of being "on the street," rather than as an original condition. Palenski's view is further substantiated in an eloquent discussion of Brazilian street children/workers by Mark Lusk who observes that ". . . even the most occasional street worker is exposed to drugs, violence and worker exploitation that characterise street culture" (1992: 297).

The interconnection between runaway youth living on the street and delinquent/illegal activity has been the subject of several studies. Kufeldt and Nimmo (1987), whose study divided 489 adolescents in the downtown core of Calgary into "runners," who have lived on the streets for an extended period of time, and into "in and outers," for whom the street was a provisional site, found that a greater percentage of runners were or had been involved in illegal activities. Such activities most frequently included street prostitution, drugs, and theft. Moreover, they also found that the majority of runners had also experienced physical and sexual abuse. A comparable study in the same year by Janus, McCormack, Burgess, and Hartman (1987), which was conducted in a Toronto shelter for runaways, similarly concluded that street experiences commonly consist of sexual abuse (a predominant factor for girls and young women) and violence, as well as interactions with the police. William McCarthy drew analogous conclusions three years later in a 1990 study, further exposing a connection between runaways and violence. Using multivariate techniques to analyze the prevalence and incidence of illegal activities associated with "living on the streets" among 390 street youth residing at several downtown Toronto shelters and common street hang-outs, McCarthy found that "a greater proportion of adolescents violate the law [in terms of theft, the selling of drug and prostitution] after they leave home (relative to the proportion of offenders at home) and offend on more than one occasion" (1).

Similarly to the Canadian studies cited here, much of the existing literature on Guatemalan and Brazilian children also emphasizes aberrant and/or unlawful activities among street children, such as petty thievery, drug use and abuse, gang violence, and prostitution (Lave, 1995; Human Rights Watch, 1997; Inciardi and Surratt, 1998; Diversi, Filho, and Morelli, 1999; UNICEF, 1999). Like Palenski's progressive sequence of activities which lead to hustling as the primary means of survival for North American street youth, Lave's (1995) investigation of Guatemalan street children suggests the more children are inculcated into street culture, the more involved they become in unlawful activity. In contrast, one particular study of Latin American street children/workers (Lusk, 1989) questions the common perception of street children as criminals and delinquents. Lusk, in fact, found that it was a minority of street children who engaged in unlawful behaviour as a means of survival, and yet this group overshadowed the majority of street children who worked legally. In further probing this issue, Lusk's 1992 study revealed that aberrant behaviour was more prevalent in street children who had severed ties with family and school.

Common challenges

I've been on and off [the street], like I've been in and out of institutions, group homes, sugar daddies, the streets, garbage dumpsters, forty below nights, the warmest place you can find is a Chinese food garbage dumpster. (Noam, Toronto, Age 22)

Street youth face numerous challenges once on the street. In my research I found a large number of young people involved in alcohol and drug use and abuse. In Canada, marijuana and heroin were commonly used and in Guatemala, glue and varsol were more prevalent. In numerous interviews, boredom, emotional pain, and suffering were cited as reasons why Canadian and Guatemalan youth engaged in such activity: "I'd run out of money and then I wouldn't eat for the remainder of the month, so that how I ended up getting into the drug scene, basically hunger, I started selling and using drugs . . ." (Tony, Age 22, Halifax). Similar findings are discussed in Diversi, Filho and Morelli's (1999) study of Brazilian street children and Lave's (1995) analysis of Guatemalan street children. Both Latin American studies highlight the sense of alienation, loneliness, and emotional trauma embedded in the drug and alcohol activities of street youth. A Guatemalan psychologist comments that the use of solvents such as glue and varsol on the streets of Latin American cities signals a deeply rooted cultural mal-aise in which "this population is attempting to forget their troubled past and irrelevant present" (Karabanow, Leman, Leveiller, and Prowse, 1997). The impact of historical and present-day oppression and systemic poverty is revealed in the following testimony of an eleven year-old Guatemalan girl who described her chronic glue-use as the "only way to survive out here [on the street] . . . it helps to make everything warm inside . . . and stops your brain from thinking bad things" (Dasa).

In addition to drug use and abuse, prostitution and petty thievery also make up some of the activities of street life, and were explained by those I interviewed as the primary ways to "make quick money." Sixteen-year-old Lois in Toronto, for instance, recounts that her day "consists of looking for something to make money off of . . . scamming, stealing and stuff . . . used to rob CN [Canadian National] trains . . . to get money to eat." Another street youth describes his story: ". . . We had an extremely co-dependent negative drug-based relationship. We both ended in Vancouver for almost a year, I got shot, and both of us were turning tricks for our habits. We led three hundred dollar a day habits for both of us, it was really nasty" (Tony, Age 22, Halifax). A Montreal adolescent tells a similar story, highlighting his very personal feelings of knowing his girlfriend was involved in prostitution:

> We stared squeegeeing which was basically enough to cover our needs for the first two months, and one day she ended up invited to do such and such in a car for X amount of dollars and she actually did. And then she came and told me about it. And I'm like well, part of me was like really thrilled because OK she had like $100 in her pocket, and like I was sick [from heroin] and I'm like cool at least we don't have to squeegee to get well bound [use heroin]. On the other hand my girlfriend just sucked some whatever to some other guy even for money and you know, I felt horribly betrayed, and so this started happen-ing more and more cause the one guy she'd see, she'd seen him five or six times. . . . (Lial, Age 19, Montreal).

For a minority of the street youth population in both North and Latin America, there is a direct correlation between addiction and illegal or de-linquent moneymaking activities. Many participants interviewed were clear in making the linkage that they needed to make "quick money" in order to feed their addictions. As such, immediate moneymaking activities for the population tended to involve prostitution, petty thievery, drug selling, and squeegeeing. Interconnected with these activities is the ever-present existence of street violence.

Violence and gang activity among street youth has also been identified in mainstream social work as a growing street phenomenon. The issue of street and gang violence, highlighted by the extraordinary occurrence of when Brazilian street youth swarmed beaches in Ipanema and robbed vacationers, has led several authors to suggest that violence within and among gangs of street youth and youth violence directed toward the public have advanced to the point of making them a central concern for law enforcement and social workers alike (Lusk, 1992; Kipke, Simon, Montgomery, Unger, and Iversen, 1997; Human Rights Watch, 1997; Inciardi and Surratt, 1998; Marquez, 1999). While violence played a small part in the street lives of those I personally interviewed (Karabanow, 1999a, 2000, 2002), one candid admission by a twenty-two-year-old Haligonian is worth mentioning: ". . . it's crazy out here [on the street] . . . violence happens . . . I've been drop kicked to the head . . . especially if you decide to do [pan] the bars . . ." (Louis).

Apart from the naming of violence in mainstream social work literature, there is a noticeable lack of contextual discussion about the inequitable and oppressive conditions affecting the lives of those who live on the street. Systemic poverty, chronic fear, and lack of genuine opportunities, as well as physical and psychological trauma combine to create only more structural barriers and injustices that are all too often invisible in the lives of homeless youth. Missing from mainstream discussions of violence among homeless youth are analyses in which violence is situated within a larger cycle of repression. While being careful not to condone violence, it is imperative for social workers and law enforcers to deal with street youth violence in all of its complexities, including understanding violence as a means for some disenfranchised youth on the streets of gaining control, of self-empowerment.

Street youth are frequently both perpetrators and victims of street violence. The streets for homeless adolescents shape a constantly changing subculture that is often animated by a dynamic of lawlessness. The homeless are subject to violence originating not only from other homeless youth, but from those whose jobs it is, more often than not, to protect. In third-world countries, most notably Brazil and Guatemala, are horrific documented accounts of harassment, torture, and murder of street children by military/paramilitary officials, local policemen, security guards, and private citizens (Americas Watch and Physicians for Human Rights, 1991; Lave, 1995; Casa Alianza, 1995; Human Rights Watch, 1997). While few cases of such repression directed towards homeless adolescents have been reported in North American cities, an increasing number of street youth in Toronto, Halifax, and Montreal have, over the past few years, testified to being harassed by local police officers and security guards. Name calling, increased ticketing for minor illegalities such as jaywalking, and being pushed, shoved, and punched have become routine fare for street youth in these Canadian cities: ". . .You've got security guards, like Spring Garden Road [Halifax], that's like the main street for making money and they'll ask you to move. I've had security guards, like when I'm sleeping behind Park Lane, I've had one kick me in the side of the head and tell me to 'get the fuck up and leave.' And like a friend of mine they beat up because he was sleeping on the stairwell" (Tom, Age 17, Halifax). Such accounts reinforce the level of marginality experienced by street youth populations.

A recent development in welfare literature is a shift in focus to the subjective experiences of street youth. There now exist an interest in the self-perceptions of homeless youth as well as a new responsiveness to an individual's comprehension of the conditions affecting their lives, and shaping their aspirations (de Oliveira, Baizerman, and Pellet, 1992; Karabanow, 1994; Karabanow and Rains, 1997; Human Rights Watch, 1997). Common experiences of many participants in my studies included "feeling alone," "having little purpose," and "not fitting in." A young Toronto street girl describes the homeless population as ". . . confused and wanting to get on the right step but can't find that step . . . they're hurt, [feel] pain, and [have] been forgotten" (Karen, Age 17). Still other participants stated that they did not feel "a part of anything," and believed that most citizens perceived them as "thieves," "criminals," and "dregs of society." These expressions of alienation and marginalization appear to characterize life on the street life for many homeless youth.

> When you out there panning [panhandling], at least note that we're there. It's not a rock on the side of the road, it's a person. It's not a rock or a chair or a bag of garbage. As much as some people like to believe it's a bag of garbage, it's a person, and that person's going through a rough time right now. . . . (Devon, Age 17, Halifax)

> We're not out there to bother people, we're just out there to try and survive. And there's a stigmatism with all homeless people that they're bad . . . they're just out there because they have to be out there . . . they're just out there to get something to eat, get money, get food, get some kind of support because they don't have anything. . . . (Lana, Age 18, Halifax)

Similarly, many young Guatemalans who were interviewed by Lave (1995) also identified themselves with varying degrees of self-awareness as "outcasts" and "street vermin," amplified by the fact that aggressive physical attacks on street children by the authorities or even the public generally go unnoticed and unresolved.

A growing concern for the physical and mental health of street youth, involved in high-risk behavior such as drug abuse and unprotected sex, and who have little or no support from adults, has also been at the center of some recent progressive studies (see for example, Lave, 1995; Inciardi and Surratt, 1998; Earls and Carlson, 1999). The street youth whom I interviewed admitted to having unprotected sexual intercourse with strangers and to indiscriminately sharing syringes. Living on the street places youth at high risk for contracting sexually transmitted diseases (STDs), including HIV, having unintended pregnancies, physical injuries, asthma, lice and scabies, sleep deprivation, depression, and attempting suicide (Canadian Pediatric Society, 1998; Ensign, 1998; Farrow et al., 1992; Weinreb et al., 1998). Noah, who lives on the street in Montreal, describes such a scenario:

> I have chronic bronchitis and I'm hepatitis C. I'm not doing so good . . . and I made another suicide attempt, very public suicide attempt I still have scars from. I did some time in the psych [psychiatric] ward and they put me on a bunch of anti-depressants and mood stabilizers and said I was schizophrenic and I was a danger to myself. And then as soon as I seemed normal they let me go . . . so I moved from the psych [psychiatric] ward directly back onto the street. (Age 19)

Noah's testimony underscores the need for supportive and affordable housing where street youth can live and continue to receive vital services once they are discharged from formal institutions such as hospitals. Unfortunately and, all too often, street youth I had sent to hospitals were later discharged directly to the streets, frequently with medications that required refrigeration and safe guarding. The dearth of adequate housing not only points to one of the many gaps in the social safety nets meted out to marginalized adolescents, but also to a general lack of public interest towards street youth. This apathy regarding the welfare of homeless adolescents has left street youth service providers in Toronto, for instance, frustrated and feeling overwhelmingly incompetent to help those who have been dumped onto the streets by hospitals and mental health centers (Karabanow, 2000; 2002). While there is no empirical evidence of growing mental health issues within the street youth population in North and Latin America, much anecdotal experiences point to a crisis in terms of young people feeling alienated, stigmatized, unhealthy, and lost—leading many front line providers to perceive the population as increasingly at risk of physical and mental health deterioration (Karabanow, 2002).

The nature and scope of emotional and psychological trauma experienced by street youth has in reality received little scholarly attention. The profound pain of abjection experienced by a majority of homeless youth as a result of their marginalization from mainstream society is often compounded by experiences of geographical displacement and separation due to war and natural disasters. Family abuse and violence, abandonment, rejection, and the wretchedness of poverty also contribute to the emotional and psychological trauma experienced by street youth, the impact of which can be seen in their educational and social development (UNICEF, 1999; Lave, 1995; Human Rights Watch, 1997). Unable to access or receive the help they need, a substantial number of street youth have either contemplated or attempted suicide either prior to or once on the street. Many youth with whom I spoke, revealed having had suicidal thoughts and, in some cases, having attempted suicide as a desperate means of escape:

> I'm dealing with a lot of issues, a lot of things have happened [at home], I moved around a lot when I was younger [in foster care], I started getting flash backs and I came to a point where I actually attempted to, I would say, do it in, attempt suicide. . . . (Leon, Age 21, Halifax)

> I don't really know what I am doing . . . I'm 21 years old, I've been through a hard life, barely had a chance of growing up to be a kid, so a lot of days I'm this 21 years old big kid. There's days when I wake up and I'm just like "yeah, o.k. where's the TV, I need to watch my cartoons" or like I'll just be hanging out with a friend and I'll just do something like maybe a seven year old would do, like just let this little kid out of me. . . . (Tom, Age 21, Halifax)

The above-mentioned challenges noted by street youth in diverse geographical settings signals the high level of despair and hopelessness facing homeless youth populations in general.

Street life as a career

Traditionally much of the literature concerning street youth has focused on topics of causality. The aim of such work has been primarily to uncover individual traits and attributes of street-entrenched youth in comparison to samples of non-street youth. More recently, however, a smaller body of work has highlighted the dimensions of street subculture, often signaling the so-called deviant and delinquent nature of street living. Absent from all of these discussions is a focus on the street youth him/herself and on the ways he or she understands, perceives and makes sense of day-to-day street life. In this section I attempt to illuminate these neglected areas of homeless culture, and in so doing, I hope to bring a humanizing perspective. My aim is to explore how homeless adolescents understand themselves and their environments from their own standpoints of young adolescents, rather than from the conventional standpoint which posits homeless youth as a unified population of "street kids" with essentialized characteristics. The following comment of a young adolescent on the streets in Montreal about one alternative street youth organization (Dans La Rue) is an instructive starting point for my thinking: "I like what is done at DLR, I mean, how they treat us . . . everybody just thinks we're street kids, bad kids, doing bad things, not here, here [DLR] we're just kids . . ." (David, Age 16).

This analysis adopts the notion of "careers" that was originally advocated by sociologists such as Howard Becker, Ervin Goffman, David Matza, and Prue Rains, in an attempt to understand how youth move toward/away from street life. These sociologists advocated for naturalistic analyses which could be "true to the nature of the phenomenon under study" (Matza, 1969:5). As such, I attempt to uncover the multiple processes of involvement in the phenomenon of street life, which include pre-stages of street life, contemplation, the period of "crossing the invitational edge" (i.e., engaging in the event in question), reworking one's image when on the street, and then for some, exiting street life. These events or sequences are told from the perspectives of youth themselves. A fundamental tenet of investigating street culture within the "career" model is recognizing the individual agency of the homeless youth who are, in effect, one's research participants. In other words, homeless youth are not objects of research, but potential research "subjects" who are able to define the meaning of their actions and decisions. Rather than identifying homeless youth as "unwilling subjects" (Matza, 1969) in their engagement in street culture, I aim to portray street youth as actively shaping their own destinies. As such, I ask participants to highlight their internal thought processes as they attempt to define their individual situations. It becomes evident throughout this section the extent to which the majority of street youth have a relatively high degree of self-awareness as they reflect upon their identities and environments.

The numbers of homeless youth I interviewed are not the commonly characterized "victims" of externalities but can be viewed as willing partakers, albeit within a limited context of restrictive and punitive social structures and institutions, in constructing their positions in the world. In other words, homeless youth like non-homeless youth participate in the myriad processes and practices which affect our lives:

> It is worthy to note that many children facing adverse circumstances portray themselves not as victims awaiting rescue but as individuals actively engaging in shaping their life courses. Far from being passive and dependent, they seek to promote their survival, forge an identity and negotiate a place for themselves in society. (Panter-Brick and Smith, 2000: 20)

In the following, I highlight some of the pivotal stages in the lives of young people who adopt and define the label of "street youth." These stages are: Pre-Entry Conditions; Contemplation; Entering Street Life; Building Identity; and, Exiting or Disengagement.

Pre-entry conditions

The existing literature has primarily focused upon the developmental stage, which deals with pre-entry conditions into street culture. Generally, empirical and anecdotal evidence has been used to support two thematic areas in discussions about homeless culture: running toward street life and running away from traumatic experiences and making the street one's home. Several authors contend that street life "pulls" some young people away from the conventional institutions of school, family, and church (D'Angelo, 1974; Green, 1998; Panter-Brick and Smith, 2000; Yablonski, 1968; Wilkinson, 1987). This perspective, which identifies the street as a source of "freedom," and "excitement," and as a remedy for "boredom," and which posits the street youth as one who "chooses his/her situation" (Green, 1998; Visano, 1990), has been largely debunked as inaccurate, superficial, and lacking in individual perspectives. While the field of social work is in dire need of extending its knowledge base to take account of the contextual and systemic dimensions of homelessness, I have found in my research a small number of street youth who view the street as an extension of their "explorations in adolescence." Seventeen-year-old Cory of Toronto said that he "needed some time out, some time to just breathe and hang and have some fun." Likewise, sixteen-year-old Stephanie of Montreal argued that "[On the street] . . . you get to do what you want, no one tells you anything, no one bothers you about what you do."

Moreover, some anecdotal evidence points to a subculture of street youth drawn to street life as a result of an attraction. Some adolescents have the notion that street life is "funky," "hip," and "cool." Twenty-one year-old Lana in Halifax: "When I was fifteen, I thought it would be cool to get away from my mom. I up and left for the night, a night out on the streets." Seasoned or "hard-core" street youth, as they say on the street, make a distinction between those on the street for legitimate reasons related to, for instance, abuse and/or poverty, and those on the street because of their perception of street life as cool and fun. The latter group has been labeled "Twinkies" by more experienced street youth:

> They're such Twinkies . . . people that don't have to be there . . . some kids who left home and didn't need to or thinks it's really cool to be down panhandling and all these little group home kids who are like "the group home is cool and I'm twelve and I'm pregnant" . . . misconceptions . . . that it's cool that you'll be partying all the time, like you'll be drunk every night . . . just the whole romanticized, little glorification of living on the street and how you and your girl, your dog are going to fucking live in this world. . . . (Sandra, Age 19, Halifax)

Another youth explains his view of the two types of youth groups on the street:

> If their home wasn't that bad . . . they just don't like the rules or something. They're spoiled all their lives, and they didn't like the rules that were being set before them. I'd tell them to stay home and deal with the rules. But if their situation was like if their parents were raping them or beating them or something, yeah leave home, or go to a shelter or something. But if it's not that bad and they just don't like the rules or something, then they should stay home and deal with it. (Blair, Age 17, Montreal)

To be sure, aspects of current popular culture like the Seattle grunge scene and the urban black hip-hop craze, for instance, have their geneses in street (or street-like) culture. As such, street life emerges as a "right of passage"—as a means of identifying one's level of toughness and ability to cope with adversity. An instructive distinction between living on or of the street can be made. Many youth on the street, especially in Guatemala, make conscious decisions (albeit within specific cultural, social, and economic contexts) to be a part of that environment. For those youth, living on the street can be a way to earn money, either for themselves or their families, as well as a place to play with others (Green, 1998; Panter-Brick and Smith, 2000): "I sell fruit in the morning here at the market so I can help out my mother, she needs money . . . after that work I stay to be with my friends here on the street . . . ya, they are all in the same situation" (Lorenzo, Age 14, Guatemala). The street for some youth instills a sense of escape and independence and, in some cases, even amusement, outside of the family (Green, 1998). The notion of young people choosing the street as a way of life, however, must be contextualized within the network of power relations which unfortunately though inevitably privilege and enable some and not others, and the problematic social structures such as those which organize child welfare and our educational systems: ". . . I floated from friend to friend and I could have went home at anytime. I didn't want to live with my dad. He was an asshole, he used to beat me around and shit . . ." (Don, Age 17, Halifax); "I admit I didn't like the rules [at home]. But I think there was more to it than just rules. It's just me and my mom could not get along and I was always getting into trouble" (Louis, Age 22, Halifax). A seventeen-year-old Toronto girl describes her choosing the street as an alternative to living with her drug-addicted parents: "When I was a little runaway kid, I guess I wanted to be, I guess I didn't want to have a house, I didn't want to have people tell me what to do . . . I had a home and I fucked it up" (Amy). The street evidently has many roles and meanings, and has been a place of work and play for young people as a result of societies' failing social practices.

Much has been written concerning the "push" factors which have been considered directly responsible for forcing youth onto the streets. As noted in the previous chapter, some "push" factors include family or child welfare placement dysfunction, physical, sexual and/or emotional abuse, and systemic poverty (Farber and Kinast, 1984; Karabanow, In press; Kufeldt and Nimmo, 1987). Often, those factors have been used to legitimize the movement of youth toward the street, with some authors and youth pointing out that the street offers a more secure, safer, and sympathetic environment than the dysfunction within certain family homes, and/or child welfare sites. "I always thought that being on the street was at least better, less dangerous than staying with my dad. I wasn't beat up every day on the street" (Chris, Age 18, Montreal). The notion of the street as a kind of refuge highlights the elements from which youth are running. More often than not, those elements pertain to the traumatic experiences of living with various kinds of abuse and neglect, with dire poverty, and with a sense of chronic individual alienation and loneliness. As remarked by an eighteen-year-old Toronto boy: "If home was good and if it was safe, I'd be back there in a minute" (Liam).

Contemplation

My research has shown that most youth regardless of the pre-entry conditions pertaining to their individual situations typically have some notion of what street culture entails prior to "crossing the invitational edge." Others, such as Visano (1990) and Baker and Panter-Brick (2000) have also made similar observations, noting that the majority of youth whom they have surveyed had contemplated escape from their present situations and imagined what awaited them on the "other side." The participants in my studies, for example, indicated they had all experienced street life in a rudimentary fashion prior to full engagement. This experimentation of sorts with street life can be considered a critical test which informs the contemplation stage. Some of the adolescents in my research reported spending whole afternoons "hanging out" with more entrenched street youth, while others experimented with sleeping on the street for one or two nights as a trial period. Still others had heard stories or gained basic information about street-based activities like prostitution, drug use/selling, and squat life prior to making a decision.

> I was off and on since I was eleven basically. I was trying to get away when I was ten years old. Running for like a day and coming back and then it got longer and I started getting older . . . I started going weeks, months at a time. (Dianne, Age 17, Montreal)

> I was 15 and thought it would be cool to be on the street. A night out on the street and I said to myself "I need to go home"—it was a rough night, it was really cold and it was really hard to fall asleep. You're freezing and you got to try and stay awake, move around a lot to keep yourself warm and it's really hard. (Toni, Age 18, Halifax)

I was just living with my dad and I was running away, so I was staying with friends every night and when I couldn't find a friend to stay with I would usually walk around the streets or something. (Will, Age 17, Toronto)

Like I had some idea of what it would be like [on the street], I don't know, just from what people were saying, like how you'd get some cash in the day so that you could pay for a room, stuff like that. (Eric, Age 15, Montreal)

Most youth also have at least some basic understanding of the support services that are available to them. Surprisingly, many young people have explicit information about the types of programs offered by the various youth shelters, drop-in centers, and health clinics. Before entering street life on a full-time basis, many young people have learnt from others where to obtain food, take a shower, or find a bed, in addition to the pros and cons of each service organization.

Everybody knows about Covenant House [Toronto youth shelter], the workers are good, they care, that you can get food bags on Tuesdays and Thursdays . . . have a bed for two weeks. . . . (Lisa, Age 16, Toronto)

I heard of the place through hearsay from other people who'd come to Toronto and they had mentioned "yeah go to the Ark man, the Ark's cool." (Tony, Age 22, Halifax)

This informal exchange of information among youth contemplating life on the street informs them of potential survival mechanisms and strategies. While some gain first-hand information by spending time directly on the street, others seek out experienced advice from perceived key informants, who might be ex-street youth, or youth presenting themselves as knowledgeable about such a culture. Service organizations such as youth shelters and drop-in centers are also locations where the exchange of street information from the seasoned street youth to the neophyte can take place. Workers in those organizations consistently note how younger, more inexperienced youth begin to "learn the ropes" of street life through interactions with more experienced members within the culture. The information obtained about street life through these unofficial channels of transmission is frequently idealized and, as a result, misleading. Nonetheless, it forms part of the basis upon which many decisions are made about "crossing the invitational edge" and becoming a youth on the street.

Within the career model, positive feelings about the future stage or next move are produced during the contemplation period if the picture of street life imagined by the youth is satisfying and corresponds to their situation of either running away from trauma or running towards freedom. For some street youth, street life is perceived as a physically and psychologically healthier place than the home or child welfare setting (Aptekar, 1988; Panter-Brick and Smith, 2000). If the street is perceived, defined or understood ultimately as providing an end to family abuse, school troubles, or individual boredom, then the next stage in the development of the street youth career will most likely be experienced. Mike, a sixteen year-old Montreal adolescent explains his escape to the street as a way of dealing with family problems:

> I couldn't really take it any more [at home], my dad was really getting on me, everything I did was just bad, it was just wrong all the time . . . ya, I thought maybe running away was the answer, I could crash at The Open Door [youth shelter], I don't know or maybe find somewhere on the street . . . anything seemed better than home.

If, on the other hand, the street is judged by an individual as impalpable, then the stage of contemplation is usually prolonged. The youth will then seek out alternative routes such as attempting to resolve conflict by talking with parents and teachers, or increasing the level of excitement in their life by seeking out and making different friends.

> I would say I had the best teacher in the world because she knew what I was going through at home. I was rebellious, when I came up to teachers, but she was one teacher, didn't matter how much I argued she always made sure that I hung in there. I would have to say that if it wasn't for her, I probably would have been a high school drop-out. (Lars, Age 21, Halifax)

> No way was I going back to the street. No way! So I was thinking there has to be other things, other ways. That's when I told my English teacher what was happening at home with my step dad. (Nancy, Age 18, Toronto)

> I stayed up the whole night [on the street]. I tried to sleep but I couldn't. I stayed up the whole night and I went home the next day and put up with another year of living at home with my mom. (Toni, Age 18, Halifax)

Rather than perceiving the move towards or away from street life as random or impulsive, the majority of street youth admit to prior contemplation and for many, periodic trials. As noted by Craig, a seventeen year-old Halifax adolescent: "It was building up for years and I thought about it and everything and then one night I bought some new shit [clothes] and then take it home and my dad takes it back and gets the money . . . and he like grabs me by my head and is smashing my head off the wooden arm of a chair . . . and smacking me around . . . and I was like 'fuck this, I can't bear this guy so I'm booking [leaving]' and I left at three in the morning and wasn't ever going back."

Home is where you make it: Entering street culture

Increasing exposure to street culture characterizes the stage of entering into street life within the career model. The experience of seventeen year-old Karen of Toronto typifies this stage in the career paradigm: "[Street] people wandering around usually come up to us and say 'we haven't seen you here before,' you know, 'when did you guys get here, where do you come from?' So we talk and just start conversing and then they show us around." Typically, the neophyte at first spends time alone adapting to his or her new surroundings. In the early phases of street living, the majority of time is spent trying to meet survival needs such as finding food and shelter and negotiating new types of social interactions (Visano, 1990 also highlights this point). As time passes most youth decide on a street tribe or set of friends who generally have similar stories of pre-entry and who have shared goals and objectives. It is within this new group the youth learns the rules of survival on the street. The stage of entering street culture takes on a quasi-apprenticeship role, whereby the novice begins to gain knowledge and experience concerning things like money-making activities, different street youth populations, street codes and rules, stories/traditions/rituals of street life, and about service providers.

> I found out about the "infirmary" [squat] because Lisa took me there to get out from the cold. I'm staying there now for almost two weeks. (Steve, Age 17, Toronto)

> I never did that [prostitution] before I ran away. Tina told me it was easy and you just had to look young. They [Tina and some other street youth] had done a [pornographic] movie because some old guy asked them if he could film them doing stuff . . . so she [Tina] told me if I ever wanted to do that she could get it set up. (Alexy, Age 17, Montreal)

The existing literature on street sub-cultures has placed much emphasis on the purported deviant aspects of street life, like drug use and selling, gang activity, prostitution, petty crimes, and violence. While these activities are for many unconventional and, for most, illegal, the notion of deviance, for some, ignores the social and economical components which shape these activities and related industries, and should therefore be excised from discussions that do not take account of an analysis of those crucial factors. Many street youth engage in illegal activities as a way to survive their daily situations: "Yes I smoke [crack], I was big [into it], well I still am, to escape reality and stuff" (Karen, Age 17, Toronto); ". . . it [drug use] takes all the emotional stuff away" (Luka, Age 13, Guatemala); "When I'm using drugs, I would use drugs to make me feel better" (Adam, Age 17, Montreal). Veale, Taylor, and Linehan (2000) suggest in their overview of the literature on street youth culture that illegal street activities are more accurately understood as coping mechanisms for difficult situations rather than as deviant or pathological vices. The experiences of those street youth I surveyed appear to support the idea of illegal activities as coping mechanisms as it was frequently explained to me that panhandling, squeegeeing, stealing, illegal drug use, and prostitution are "things you got to do to get by" and "part of being on the street." Several youth also suggested the combination of boredom and low self-esteem as reasons for involvement in illegal activities:

> I find that being homeless and having so much time on your hands, I don't know, you mostly fall into the drug scene. We don't have a lot of self respect so you don't shower a lot, or take care of yourself, or wash your clothes a lot. (Karen, Age 17, Toronto)

Often ignored in the street youth literature are those who are employed within the formal economy. Approximately one third of the street youth I surveyed were employed in low-wage service jobs that ranged from furniture movers, wait staff, bouncers, bartenders, club dancers, teleconferencing, to intermittent employment. The majority of street youth, however, were employed in the informal economy in jobs as newspaper sellers, food hawkers, shoe shiners, people "flying a sign" (walking the streets/highways with sign stating "will work for food"), squeegees, and as various street performers, including cartoonists, comedians, and acrobats. Notably, many youth spoke of the significance of working on the street:

> I don't like street loading. I don't like free loading. I don't like to free load, that's part of the reason why I prefer squeegeeing over panhandling. 'Cause even though it's a pointless labor, I can still rationalize it to myself that I'm working. It boosts my ego and my morale a bit, knowing "hey I worked for this." (Tony, Age 22, Halifax)

Hustling for money, by which youth explore both legal and illegal avenues, also occupies a lot of one's time on the street: "I was hustling the streets and that became the way to live you know. You panhandle on the corner by day and you take a cruise to the mall and you might be able to pull a trick two or three times if you're lucky" (Louis, Age 22, Halifax). Additionally, time is spent looking for places to get food and safe shelter: "I had to panhandle to make some food, money for food. Then I look for places to sleep . . . parking lots or anywhere I could sleep where it was warm" (Trevor, Age 19, Halifax). Seventeen year-old Tina in Montreal describes her daily schedule this way:

> I would wake up and walk around the whole city. I would either pan for money, pick up pennies that I see on the ground and I'd root through garbage looking for food . . . I'd start looking for my next place to sleep. And somewhere to put my stuff and if I couldn't find it then I'd walk around all night long.

According to the information I have collected, locating food is the main priority for youth on the street. Nineteen-year-old Nicko in Halifax comments that

> The hardest part [of street life] was eating. Nine times out of ten I would go around looking through people's compost trying to find the freshest thing. I'd just eat that and if there was no compost I'd look through the garbage and if their garbage wasn't any good I'd go to a fast food restaurant and go through their compost and stuff.

Less attention has been accorded to street youth activities that are not illegal or that do not relate to street survival strategies and routines. One activity that has been neglected is play. It is not uncommon in Guatemala to witness street children engaged in games of tag or having water fights in a city's busy downtown core. Outside of work and work related activities, street youth typically spend time relaxing and hanging out with friends. Many street youth, in fact, resemble non-street adolescents when they talk about the non-work related aspects of their lives. Street youth, for instance, express concerns about personal relationships, have opinions regarding daily political, social and cultural events, and make observations about daily life. When I worked with Montreal street youth, I was constantly reminded of the vulnerability of humanity. Once, for example, the leader of a hard-core street gang asked to see me in private. When we found a confidential place in the shelter, he shared the feelings he had for a new girlfriend, wanting advice on the type of gift he might give her after dating for only a short while. A similar expression of hope and desire, two basic elements of the human condition, came from an immigrant girl in Toronto who I remember shared personal stories of her home life in Honduras and told of how she used to dream of becoming a pop singer. These vignettes highlight the youth rather than street qualities of young people living on the street. Like their non-street counterparts, youth on the streets also have dreams and wishes for a good life, which for some, comes with a stable job, a family, and a home: "I want to grow up and be a counselor, help other kids on the street" (Ted, Age 19, Toronto); "Five years from now I'm hoping to be a recreational therapist in a seniors' complex" (Fred, Age 21, Halifax); "I'm pretty sure that I want to live in the country with a wife, some kids and lots of animals" (Lars, Age 14, Montreal); "I want to be able to have some land, a family, and a job" (Tola, Age 13, Guatemala).

Travel also contributes to street life experiences. Approximately half of the Canadian participants in my research, in contrast to a very small number in Guatemala, told stories about traveling, most notably, hitch-hiking, which was for most, a way to get to and from Canada's larger centers, such as Vancouver, Toronto, Montreal, and Halifax. Reasons for travel included leaving problematic situations such as owing money to drug dealers, seeking out what is perceived as more adequate resources such as youth moving to Toronto where it is thought there are more shelter beds, joining various communities like when several youth moved to Montreal to join the large squatter community, and for simply a change of scenery. Karen, a seventeen-year-old Toronto girl who recently arrived in Halifax with her boyfriend explains their scenario:

> We got kind of sick of Toronto; I kept getting drunk and getting in trouble with the cops. I was getting really sick of Toronto. And I keep getting into shit here . . . I have so many friends here . . . there's a lot more resources in Toronto [than Halifax] and there's a lot more harassment from cops . . . we needed to get away . . . people told me it was nice here [Halifax].

Indeed, for many homeless youth, life on the street is an intermittent stage in their individual development; time out and away from difficult situations. Alongside the apparent benefits of a street lifestyle or career, such as freedom from previous problems, a sense of independence and excitement, and having a sense of control, most youth on the streets are aware of the inherent dangers associated with street culture, including violence, addiction, increased trauma, illness and disease, loneliness, and in some instances, death:

> I've witnessed one girl almost get raped one night when I was on the streets. She was only about fifteen years old. She was just walking around trying to make some money so she could have something to eat and these guys come up to her and start pushing her around. (Nicko, Age 19, Halifax)

For many youth, the dangers of street life are witnessed first hand. Because of their exposure to the dangers on the streets, street youth sometime portray a well developed sense of responsibility and maturity in terms of being able to identify the strengths and limitations of their situations that surpasses that of their non-street counterparts. As one young Toronto man noted, "I see the good and bad on the streets" (Tom, Age 20). Often when future aspirations are noted by street youth, an even greater sense of self-awareness is realized, highlighting a key stage in developmental psychology in which one attempts to make sense of her or his life, as well as impart meaning to it.

In contrast, some street youth do live abject existences in which they are isolated and essentially disconnected from mainstream institutions. Youth living this way are the most difficult to reach and others on the street manage a variety of associations with aspects of mainstream culture. All too often street youth culture is depicted as an isolated, singular entity. More accurately, street youth live within "domains of complementarity," among family, school, and service providers (Lucchini, 1996). While much has been written about the lack of structure on the street (Karabanow, 1994; Karabanow and Rains, 1997), street youth share a different version. Life on the street for some youth can be highly structured around times to visit family, to earn money working (e.g., panhandling, squeegee, prostitute, sell drugs, petty thievery), to play, find accommodation in a squat, in a secluded outdoor space, or at a shelter, to enjoy a shower at a drop-in center, and around the need to be on time at a shelter to obtain dinner or a food bag at a food bank or a mobile service provider. Street lives are also organized around social activities like parties, movies, drug and alcohol use, and sex.

In her analysis of alcoholics, Wiseman (1970) coined the apt term "making the loop" to identify the paths traveled by her research participants through the network of available services. Many street youth described a similar routine:

> Usually there are three [meals] from the Brunswick Street United Church. There's a breakfast program in the morning, then you can go to ARK [drop-in] at ten and eat and then some days ARK's open again at four for supper. So, you know, some days you can get three meals in. (Trevor, Age 19, Halifax)

Street youth are usually aware of the daily options available to them. Some visit family or friends (outside of the street) on a regular basis, others return to school on a part-time basis, while most have some contact with the multitude of service providers set up to help them (Panter-Brick and Smith, 2000). Veale, Taylor, and Linehan (2000) concur that "in reality, children exist within multiple communities, and their experience is one of moving between different settings in the street and their community of origin" (141). For some street youth, street life is generally perceived as a social event, far from being an isolating and unstructured experience.

> I get to see everybody [on the street], Sal [boyfriend] is always with me . . . even my dad came to see if I needed any money and there's a lot of social workers that come down to the park a lot. (Dianne, Age 17, Montreal)

> . . . My father now still doesn't let me live with him, he still can't accept that I'm gay, but he does give me money every two weeks. (Stewart, Age 21, Halifax)

> I slept on the streets and then I would go and find a friend and live there and if that didn't work out go back on the streets for a couple of days and either go back home and live and wait for a bed to open up at Phoenix [youth shelter]. (Lana, Age 19, Halifax)

It seems that for a minority of street youth, who seriously engage in illegal activity such as drug use and prostitution, and activities linked to gangs, they begin to identify through such activities and as a result have less standardized contact with mainstream organizations (Baker and Panter-Brick, 2000; Visano, 1990). Nevertheless, even this hard-core segment of youth still maintain some contacts (albeit minimal) with service providers and family members (Karabanow, 1999a).

Building identity

Young people become involved in the processes which eventually lead to a life on the street at varying stages in their individual development. While it is imperative for social workers and youth service providers to recognize the inequities and special circumstances that may be produced by the many differences between and among youth and others, it is equally important to acknowledge the active participation of youth in shaping their personal identities, and how they comprehend the world around them. Far from simply adopting the stereotypes of victim and/or criminal that have been scripted by others, most street youth perceive themselves quite differently.

For some, who have escaped dangerous situations (primarily within abusive families and relationships), they identify themselves as heroes and survivors, while others view themselves as explorers and travelers of new territory: "I think of myself as not a homeless person because we can survive, we make money somehow, right, so we ain't really homeless. I think of myself as not homeless cause I can survive on my own" (Luke, Age 16, Halifax). The majority of street youth I met recognized having an amount of agency in the events and processes that brought them to their present conditions. They were also aware of their roles in re-constructing their identities as "homeless," "punk," or "gangster," preferring these over the stereotypes linked to notions of powerlessness and self-alienation. When asked to describe themselves, many youth used words like "caring," "good," "loyal," "brave," and "trustworthy," which mirror the findings repeatedly noted by Panter-Brick and Smith (2000) in their work with abandoned children. Significantly, self-identification acts as a barometer which measures the degree of youth entrenchment in street culture. For those who perceive themselves in conflict with mainstream culture, using names like "addict" and "gang banger," to describe themselves, the harder it is for them to re-integrate into mainstream society. On the other hand, youth who see themselves as "survivors" and as "healthy," have had less difficulty in separating themselves from street culture (this will be discussed below). For example, the majority of street children in Guatemala see themselves not as "street people" but as "family helpers"—attempting to accrue some extra money for their family group. On the other hand, a small minority of very entrenched street children in Guatemala have shedded the "helping" image and identify more with the street's unconventional lifestyle (such as prostitution, drug selling, and thievery).

In the process of shaping their identities, discarding as well as reviving stereotypes, and creating new monikers, homeless youth are acutely aware of how others perceive them, evident in the ways in which they present themselves to the public. Panhandlers, for instance, sometimes attempt to elicit sympathy from passersby, while gang members aim to project a tough image to outsiders. It is now more common to see some young people carrying self-made cardboard signs describing their predicaments (such as "need bus fare to return home;" "will work for food" or "want to pay my rent") and marking their identities on the street. Moreover, some street youth have a general awareness of the networks of experts interested in their situations—from public health officials to juvenile justice workers, to guidance counselors, social workers, and youth workers. Because street youth do in fact constitute a number of groups who frequently fall within the jurisdictions of the courts, the police, the social worker, the teacher, the local merchant, as well as the parent, they sometimes misinterpret the attention they receive as a kind of power belonging to them inherently because of their homeless condition.

> It's sort of funny how many people want to know what I do, there's my probation officer and like the judge I guess, all the workers at The Open Door [youth shelter], it's like I'm real popular. . . . (Dennis, Age 16, Montreal)

While homeless youth are indeed the center of attention for many within our societies, the power which street youth sometimes recognize is part and parcel of the myriad relations and practices which organize any regulatory system, including social work, the law, and education.

More recently, street youth have become the focus of study for academics and a popular topic in the media. For some street youth, this much-required attention has had the unfortunate effect of creating the impression of being special, unique and/or important for reasons that are inadequately understood. Throughout my work experiences at youth shelters in Toronto, Montreal, Halifax, and Guatemala, I rarely had to persuade an adolescent to share her or his story with a journalist, a researcher, or myself. Usually, youth were more than enthusiastic about any opportunity to talk about themselves. The exclamation of sixteen-year-old Jay in Toronto illustrates this point: "I've been interviewed for the news before and for radio and stuff like that, about homelessness, drug use, stuff like that. I guess I'm some kind of expert." Such occasions to (re)present themselves to others constitute significant rarified experiences in the lives of those marginalized and disempowered members of society, among whom we find homeless youth. Lamentably, the valuable self-empowering experiences had by some street youth to tell their own stories in their own words, usually during encounters with researcher and media personalities, are rarely noted in conventional social work and social policy literature.

Typically, once an adolescent begins to lead a street "career," they quickly become familiar with the network of services offered in their surrounding areas and elsewhere. It has been argued that this industry of caring and altruistic providers can inadvertently provide a structured living arrangement (e.g., periods to sleep, eat, shower, find clothes, work on resumes, job search, meet counselors, etc.), considered beneficial by some, and unintentionally make street life a viable option (Visano, 1990; Wiseman, 1970): "But see in Toronto, you can't starve, there's places to eat every hour" (Linda, Age 18, Toronto). Logically, however, the viability of a "successful" street career largely depends on the number and quality of resources available for young people. Youth in Toronto and Montreal, for example, spoke of the relative ease in receiving food, shelter, and other supports while those in Halifax and Guatemala expressed having great difficulty in finding resources: "In [Halifax] it's different, there is the one church thing at five when you can eat and that's about it really" (Trevor, Age 19, Halifax). Yet again, the regimented atmospheres and standardized rules of the majority of service organizations frequently enhance one's sense of homelessness:

Well right now I'm at the Phoenix youth shelter and normally the wake-up call is 8:00 a.m., then you have your hour to shower, get your breakfast, and then you're out by 9:15 a.m. Then you have to stay out of the shelter until noon. I'm still homeless in a way. Then you go back to eat from 12:00 until 1:15 p.m., then you got to be out again. (Tom, Age 21, Halifax)

You get woken up at six in the morning and got to be out by seven. That's what I hated about the shelters, you know, "hello I'm sick, I'm puking, I have a fever and you're kicking me out in the cold." That's what I hated. So at least at my squats or under the bridge I could sleep and rest even though I was freezing to death. (Darcy, Age 16, Montreal)

Because my time was up in the shelter, I had no where else to go, so the only option was with a sleeping bag on the pavement. (Chris, Age 16, Halifax)

When I had to sleep in back laneways of buildings and stuff, that's when I really found out that I was homeless. And when I had to walk around all night just because I didn't have a place to sleep, waiting for the ARK to open so I could sleep there for awhile. (Trevor, Age 19, Halifax)

In locales where there is a "loop" of services (such as in Toronto and Montreal), which offer a diversity of environments, cultures, and moods, youth can shop for a location where they feel understood by the service providers there.

> I stay at Cov [Covenant House] because it's a good environment. You feel welcomed, it's not a dump or anything, the food is good and also they [staff] take care of you. (Sophie, Toronto, Age 17)

> Well this place [youth shelter] is the best, well because you can come and talk with staff; they help me with my homework. It's clean and healthy, they feed you, compared to some other shelters this is a palace. It feels like home. (Kevin, Age 17, Toronto)

As such, youth seek out services that seem to match their self-image. Some youth accept services that highlight the harshness of their past experiences, while others prefer services that illuminate their strengths living on the street. Still others are drawn to services which attempt to "fix" their troubles. This demonstrates that street youth continue to be active in defining their situations and identities, even when they need to portray certain characteristics such as deference, gratitude and/or interest, or a willingness to change in order to receive services. This conscientious representation of one's identity to others has been described as "client work" (Spencer, 1994). A good example of the strengths of self-definition comes from Susan Ruddick's (1996) study of homeless youth in Hollywood, in which she identifies the struggles by street youth to shape services into "simulated families" (Karabanow and Rains, 1997) in sites where they were identified as youth rather than as homeless people.

Disengagement/exiting street culture

The street can provide immediate benefits to adolescents seeking solutions to their problems both real and perceived. These benefits might include a social support system, safety from previous trauma, a sense of control and personal power, and freedom/independence. Many of the participants in my study highlighted the feeling of community that often exists on the street:

> We all look out for each other. Like if someone's giving us a hard time we stick up for each other and it's like the main community outside of being homeless. We have a community within the homeless community who we look out for. We talk to each other and if we need a place to stay then there may be a building that has a heater that's warm. We look out for each other

when a new person comes out on the street and we try to help them out as much as we can. (Frank, Age 21, Halifax)

We take care of each other. If any of my friends ever need anything, I'm right there for them, especially if you're a girl. Most of their friends are guys who take care of them. If a girl is with a guy and that's her boyfriend, then he and all his friends will take care of her. (Kim, Age 17, Montreal)

I was kind of lost. I got by and I met some really cool people [on the street] and sort of formed a brotherhood type thing and we all looked out for each other. That's how I survived. (Abe, Age 18, Toronto)

While many do speak of community, the majority of youth living on the street claim to "rely on themselves to survive," and are cautious in "trusting many street people." According to nineteen-year-old Steward in Montreal, "in the end, nobody looks out for you, you got to look out for yourself. It's very lonely." As one young Halifax man acknowledged, "there's a lot of good people that live on the street, good people, but there's a lot of people out there that would just snake and rip you off, take everything you got" (Trevor, Age 19). These sentiments are amplified in an eleven-year-old Guatemalan street girl's statement: "It's very lonely here on the street, nobody wants to care for you . . . you have to be independent, look after yourself because nobody will care for you . . . that's the way the street is" (Mira). As such, any notion of street community is fraught with ambiguity and complexity.

Ultimately, for the majority, any benefits derived from the street are short lived. Most experience many of the limitations of living on the street, including violence, new forms of trauma, hunger, disease and illness, exploitation and boredom: "I don't want to live on the streets in Halifax, because I know what it does to my morale and to my self-esteem, and I know that I'll just get fucked up again" (Joanne, Age 20, Halifax). Even the homeless youth who initially perceived the street optimistically, eventually experience a sense of disenchantment, which usually stems from some sort of street crisis (Visano 1990 highlights a similar pattern): "I've had a lot of bad experiences mostly when I was younger on the streets. From a lot of bad experiences I learned not to trust a lot of people" (Karen, Age 17, Toronto). One young Montreal girl recounted the trauma of being gang-raped as a prerequisite to joining a certain gang. A seventeen-year-old boy told of being beaten by a group of street youth because they wanted his leather jacket. As such, the "magic" of street life soon fades, revealing a more realistic and, frequently, sinister picture:

After a while, it was about two months; I didn't want to be here [on the streets] anymore. I was scared more and more. I wasn't getting along with the other people on the street, and I missed my old friends. (Jacquie, Age 15, Montreal)

Sooner or later, for a great many homeless youth, the street becomes increasingly associated with negative connotations, which lead many youth to reassess their current situations. In contrast to initial impressions which posited street life as a source of independence, greater personal power, and safety, street life ultimately, for most, becomes equated with boredom, excessive drug abuse, lack of sleep, hunger, extreme tiredness, and to an overall unhealthy lifestyle: "I don't think I can handle it anymore, lying down on the concrete sleeping. It's hard enough sleeping in concrete stairwells, but I'd rather sleep there than sleep outside" (Trevor, Age 19, Halifax); "It's pretty hard; there was a time when I was going to school and living on the streets, I was sleeping in banks, doing my homework in Tim Horton's [coffee shop], seeing if I could make money for a bus ride in the morning, go sleep in a bank . . . it was insane" (Mat, Age 20, Toronto); "You hardly get any sleep when you are sleeping on the streets, cause the pavement is hard, it is cold out, there is traffic noise, and the police bother you all the time" (Luke, Age 16, Halifax). One Guatemalan youth envisioned returning to jail rather than spending any more time on the streets since there he would be provided with regular meals and a bed. These negative descriptions of life on the street speak of the types of experiences which ultimately trigger the long slow process of disengagement from street culture.

As one's initial identity of hero or survivor begins to make less sense, the street youth experiences a mounting need for a new identity, and many seek outside assistance with the process of developing a new self-awareness. Concomitantly, street adolescents generally seek greater contact with people from mainstream culture, and more intimate relationships with family members and/or service providers as they become disillusioned with street life.

Maybe it's maturity, I'm getting older you know and maybe the street is too much for me now, I don't know, but me and Carlton [social worker] talk a lot about this. (Stewart, Age 19, Montreal)

So I hung out with Whane [street worker] just because I was interested in the type of work he was doing [harm reduction dissemination]. And I was interested in becoming a peer [counselor], so he hooked me up with a place called Queen West Community Center in Toronto. It brought my self esteem up, and it made me feel like I was actually doing something productive for once, you know. (Tony, Age 22, Halifax)

Another common approach to exiting street life entails "getting away" or distancing oneself from harsh street environments as a means to "cool out" and "clean up:"

> The whole point was to get me out of Toronto, because for the last year all I was doing is squeegeeing at Front [street] and Spadina [street], Front [street] and University [street]. Grinding $150 a day and it's all going up in smoke, so you know, it's not good for my lungs. It's just not healthy, and it was killing me and ruining my mind, I was starting to go insane. (Tony, Age 22, Halifax)

> I just come out here to get away from all my other friends who use, because I'm not going to be able to quit [heroin] if all my buddies are like "hey man, let's go make a wake-up [first toke of the day]." (Andrew, Age 19, Toronto)

> I figure the main thing on the line is the fact that the whole geographic change, it's away from all the negative influences that have been screwing me for the last five years. And the people I do know out here [Halifax] all don't use hard drugs. The people I do know seem to have gotten their shit together actually. (Jeremy, Age 19, Halifax)

The next two examples demonstrate maturity and an experienced perspective which appears encased with great awareness. One homeless youth who is also an immigrant to Montreal suggests one can find strength in their convictions of "having a goal," and in their determination to seek help:

> I feel confident about myself because I'm determined. I think if you really work hard for it you'll get through. You've got to put that input in it. You've got to find resources where you can ask people for help. (Dali, Age 18)

A Halifax youth spoke of leaving his gang affiliation after learning his girlfriend was pregnant and he would need to be a responsible father: "I didn't want to end up in jail or end up in a casket buried under the ground not being able to watch my son grown up. I couldn't do it" (Sacha, Age 22).

With increasing estrangement from the streets, the adolescent begins to see her/himself less as a street kid and more as an average adolescent, "friend," "son/daughter," "client," or "punk/hippie/anarchist":

> Well I just got tired of it, being a street kid. One day I had a gram [of dope] in my hand and I threw it away and said I had enough. I just found that my life

was coming to an end if I kept this up, and I was worried about my life. I thought I might get shot or something. I thought I was going to get into crimes and stuff to make some money, so I just stopped living on the streets and I put myself together. (Stan, Age 18, Montreal)

While those who stay or return to street life identify themselves more with "being a street kid," others begin to identify as "ex-street youth," "student," or "employee":

When I started to work at the shop [recycling plant], I didn't have time to see my old friends [on the street]. I'm working a lot of hours and I'm pretty tired when I finish so I go home after work or get a beer with some of my new friends [at the recycling plant]. (Ian, Age 20, Toronto)

I don't see myself as a street kid any longer, you know, I consider myself a writer. (Don, Age 19, Halifax)

As such, other defining elements of the individual's sense of self gradually emerge as dominant characteristics.

Yet another incentive to exiting street life occurs for some street youth when they realize how others define them. Some youth begin to disassociate with street life once they experience the negative, stigmatizing, and often abusive reactions from many in mainstream culture. Most street youth participants in my research expressed occasional embarrassment on the street, especially when a passerby would comment derogatively about "getting a job" or "taking a shower": "The public sees me as homeless and that I just use drugs all the time and I just use the money for drugs . . . most of them [passersby] say that" (Luke, Age 16, Halifax); "I got looked down for being homeless, for being a street kid, for being a squeegee kid, I got looked down for that" (Karen, Age 17, Toronto). In another instance I was in the process of filming street children in Guatemala when a middle-aged businessman approached me and in a scolding manner (and in front of the children) commented that I was wasting my time with such "garbage." After this incident, several street children noted that this was a common perception of the public towards their plight.

The recognition of street youth's marginalized status often results in further recognition of alternative potential identities to which youth might aspire. Several street boys whom I met in Montreal asked if I could find a detoxification center for them because they had "had enough" with strangers shouting at them to get off the street and "do something with their lives." Another youth recounts the humiliation of feeling like she had a "disease" when "mothers took their kids and pulled them closer when I walked by" (Karen, Age 17, Toronto). The ostracism described by some street youth reflects David Matza's (1969) notion of ban—the bedevilment from others.

Howard Becker's (1953) influential research on the stages of becoming a marijuana user highlights an important aspect of engagement in unconventional, usually illegal street careers. Becker suggests that motivation and commitment to deviance is fostered during the course of involvement in such an activity, rather than prior to engagement. In this light, the seeds of disengagement are also planted within the process of involvement, when the self slowly reconstructs a different set of identities. Youth on the street who do not see themselves as "street kids" experience a form of identity dissonance. As such, one's motivation and commitment shift from engagement to disengagement:

> I didn't want to do the stuff I was doing; dope selling, a lot of panhandling. I decided I needed to get out of it. It felt like I was wasting my time, it didn't feel good anymore. (Quinn, Age 19, Toronto)

> It's kind of my fault I was on the street so young, I shouldn't have been. If I see a little eleven years old on the street, you know, I take them and I'm like "go home, you don't know what you're getting yourself into, you're getting yourself stuck." (Karen, Age 17, Toronto)

Importantly, the individual still retains control of the identity construction process—attempting to satisfy the desire to become something other than a street youth. Nonetheless, individuals outside of street culture usually play pivotal roles in the stage of disengagement and identity transformation, acting as mentors and role models: "I have people look at me and tell me that they're surprised by the way I've turned out because of what I've been through. But I was able to find, thank God, the right people, the right programs and get out of that [street life]" (Simon, Age 21, Halifax).

Disengagement, like engagement, deals with attitudes and perceptions. When the streets no longer provide a sense of escape or pleasure, then transformation of meaning is required in order to develop a new conception of street life. This process occurs both internally, as the individual contemplates other options or rethinks motives, and externally through interactions/contacts with mainstream culture.

Agency and street careers

The vast majority of literature about street youth has focused on etiology and street culture with very little attention placed on the personal experiences of "being" a street youth. Few studies have attempted to account for the feelings, experiences, and sense of identity and meaning construction of street youth, as a way of extending our collective understanding of street culture and of how young people end up there.

By viewing street life as a career, I have attempted to illuminate the attitudes and experiences of adolescents as they move throughout the various stages of street life. As a way of circumventing trauma and other problematic experiences, street life takes on an almost paradisal quality, which, for most, soon fades after experiencing unexpected traumatic, frightening/dangerous, and even simply too many unpleasant events. Negative experiences prompt occasions for rethinking the viability of street life, and alternative options like the possibility of returning home, or entering a shelter are weighed. As such, this analysis highlights how the street youth "mediates the process of becoming" throughout their many personal transformations (Matza, 1969). Engagement and disengagement are related processes that are both crafted by the individual as she or he makes sense of their environment. In other words, the street youth plays the central role in the process of identity construction throughout the stages of becoming both a "street youth" and an "ex-street youth."

Such findings are useful to service providers in identifying the various stages of street youth careers and, more importantly, in acknowledging the pivotal role of the individual in scripting her or his street experiences. As noted by Miguel, a fifteen-year-old Toronto boy: "I know I have to get off the street so I don't die here, but I just got to wait for the right time." While there may exist some redeeming aspects to street life (such as independence, freedom, a sense of community and support), for the vast majority of children, this lifestyle offers a problematic and unhealthy existence. Consequently, the last twenty years has witnessed a growing industry of nongovernment and nonprofit organizations that have assumed the cause of youth homelessness. The following chapter focuses on those organizations and their programs.

Who's Helping? A Look at Organizational Responses to Street Youth

The past two decades have witnessed an intense development of organizations and programs aimed at supporting and rehabilitating street youth. These organizations range from emergency shelters, to drop-in centers, outreach services, health clinics, alternative schools, job training programs, and to medium-to-long-term supportive housing establishments. By far, the most prominent human service unit has been the emergency shelter, which generally accommodates many of the above-mentioned programs and services (Karabanow and Clement, 2004). This chapter will look at the nature and characteristics of different programs and services that are currently available to street youth.

The youth shelter

Many authors have acknowledged the youth shelter as central to the street youth's world (Karabanow, 1994; Ruddick, 1996; Snow and Anderson, 1993). My experience as a youth worker in several Canadian and Guatemalan cities supports the belief that shelters are an important stop in the travels of many street youth. Metropolitan Toronto alone has at least ten street youth shelters, while Los Angeles County in the United States increased their number of emergency shelter beds from 82 to 124, and their long-term-living beds from 0 to 88 between 1986 and 1989 (Yates, Pennbridge, Swofford, and Mackenzie, 1991:559). Similarly, Guatemala City presently accommodates thirteen diverse residential settings for homeless youth.

Surprisingly, in contrast to popular belief, the largest response to the phenomenon of street youth has come from private charities, religious groups, and nonprofit agencies (Baum and Burnes, 1993; Cooper, 1987; So-larz, 1992; Weinreb and Rossi, 1995). Henry's (1987) analysis of voluntary shelters in Washington, DC, noted that all but two organizations serving homeless people had a religious auspice, sponsorship, origin, and/or ideal. The 1988 Housing and Urban Development (HUD) national survey of homeless shelters in the United States found that 90% of all shelters are privately operated (Jencks, 1994:160).

The current taxonomy used in our health professions posits street youth as "deserving" of a genuine response to their situations. The result of this compassionate or liberal classification has been an emergence of shelters as a developing business, not only to house, but to treat street youth[1] (Tiernan, Horn, and Albelda, 1992). In contrast to most adult shelters, shelters for youth place a greater emphasis on counseling. Because youth shelters aim to "work with clients" by way of redirecting youth away from the streets, towards safer and more productive lifestyles (Karabanow and Rains, 1997), treatment becomes a major focus of youth shelters (see Abbott and Blake, 1988; Bronstein, 1996; Morrissette and McIntyre, 1989). According to Hasenfeld's (1972) continuum of organizational typologies, in which the types of "people-sustaining–people-processing–people-changing" are linked, adult shelters tend to fluctuate between the "people-sustaining" and "people-processing" categories, while youth shelters are more often char-acterized as "people-changing" institutions. In their comparative analysis of different systems of youth care, Street, Vinter and Perrow (1966) explain the idea of "people-changing":

> All complex organizations use people to pursue their tasks, but people-changing organizations work not only with or through people but also on them. People constitute the raison-d'être of these organizations, and, as our label suggests, the desired product is a new or altered person. (3)

In other words, the goal of the street youth shelter is to reintroduce its population into society as functional and productive citizens.[2]

During the past few years, academics have turned their focus toward street youth shelters, documenting "what goes on" within specific agencies from the perspectives of both youth and workers (Karabanow and Rains, 1997; Kariel, 1993; Ruddick, 1996). The resulting literature from this new academic interest in youth shelters has been generally more redeeming than what we have learned from adult shelters, portraying a "culture of care" (Karabanow and Rains, 1997), wherein attempts to recreate family-like environments with friendly and understanding staff are made (Karabanow, 1994; Kariel, 1993; Ruddick, 1996; Washton, 1974). The present categorization of street youth as "deserving" has informed such studies for the last few decades.[3]

Youth shelters, however, have also been criticized on the grounds that they resemble correctional institutions through an excess of rules, rigid structures, and "power hungry" staff (Abbott and Blake, 1988; Karabanow, 1994; McCarthy, 1990; Weber, 1991). It has been considered that youth shelters, like some correctional institutions, employ untrained workers as professionals (Robertson, 1992; Rothman, 1991), and are often ineffective according to staff and residents (Alleva, 1988; Kufeldt and Nimmo, 1987; Michaud, 1988; Miller, Miller, Hoffman, and Duggan, 1980; Price, 1989; Rothman, 1991). As one Toronto street girl stated about her move from a youth shelter to the street: "The shelter seemed a lot like a group home and I just had too many negative associations with the whole authority thing. So I moved from the shelter directly onto the street" (Dorothy, Age 18).

Specific segments of the street youth population, such as those aged twelve to fifteen, immigrants, refugees, Aboriginal and Black youths, drug and/or alcohol addicted youths, youths experiencing mental health issues, and gay and lesbian adolescents, generally require additional support in order to avoid being "left behind" and/or "ignored" by service providers (Karabanow, 2000). In earlier research, I have tried to highlight the existing gaps in social service networks which exacerbate the vulnerabilities of many homeless youth. My analysis of two Toronto youth shelters, for example, uncovered a common practice undertaken in mental health clinics and acute care hospitals to prematurely refer street youth to youth shelters due to a lack of adequate resources to deal with homelessness themselves (Karabanow, 2000; 2002).

Health services and street youth

Research that has focused specifically on health care services in relation to street youth has highlighted the long-established schism between these two social worlds. In a roundtable discussion with various Canadian service providers, the Canadian Pediatric Society (1998) found that most health services are not designed and delivered with street youth in mind. A significant barrier to the effective utilization of health care services by street youth, for instance, is a strong suspicion and/or dislike for conventional medical resources because they are perceived as not user-friendly (Geber, 1997; Klein et al., 2000). Several research accounts reveal that street youth are regularly "turned away" from doctors' offices and emergency hospital units because they lack identification (especially health cards) and a permanent address (Canadian Pediatric Society, 1998; Farrow et al., 1992; Klein et al., 2000). Other barriers to access to health services for street youth include: extensive waiting times; the requirement of advanced booking; the fear that parental permission will be necessary (especially for minors); a sense that health care facilities do not address their medical needs; a lack of familiarity with local health care resources; mistrust of adults/professionals due to past negative experiences; reluctance to use services outside core street youth area; and, a perceived lack of sensitivity and respect, prejudice and discrimination from health care professionals for being a "street kid" (Canadian Pediatric Society, 1998; Ensign, 1998; Farrow et al., 1992; Geber, 1997; Klein et al., 2000; Weinreb et al., 1998).

The following anecdotal account is an excellent example of these findings: In the fall of 1996, I accompanied Simon, a seventeen-year-old, seasoned street youth to the hospital after two large infected blisters formed on the middle of his left arm—a common result of using unclean needles. Simon had been using heroin throughout the summer. When we arrived at a downtown hospital's emergency desk, we were told to wait until a doctor was available. Simon appeared to be in excruciating pain—he could not move his arm and was softly crying. After one hour, I approached the nurses' desk and asked if there was any chance of having someone look at Simon's arm. The nurse replied that "he [would] have to wait; after all, it [was] his own damn fault for injecting himself. Why doesn't he go to his dealer now?" Four hours later, Simon's infections were drained of pus and his arm was bandaged. The doctor turned to me and said, "I won't do this again if he comes; my job is not to clean up his wound so he can go out and use [heroin] in an hour." When we left the hospital, Simon exclaimed, "Next time, I'll just fix it [my arm] myself—why be treated like an animal here."

School and street youth

The traditional educational system has also been the target of criticism similar to that lobbied against mainstream health services. The majority of street youth, we now know, come from problematic family backgrounds that are beset by separations, neglect, and abuse, and have further experienced placement breakdowns and poverty which inform and exacerbate educational failure (Raychaba, 1987; Snow and Findlay, 1998).

Homeless youth speak about difficulties at school as they attempt to understand and deal with their personal and familial trauma and marginalization. Many struggle with both "functional" literacy issues (such as problems in learning, difficulty reading and writing) and "critical" literacy issues (linking what they are learning to how they understand the world around them) (Freire, 1985). Learning literacy skills is hampered for homeless youth by such personal factors as low self-esteem, attachment difficulties, transient lifestyles, poverty, trauma, and learning disabilities. Added to these issues is the enormous strain on street youth brought about by the struggles of daily survival. More often than not, "teens who end up on the street rarely leave behind them stellar academic careers; most homeless youth regard school as a dirty word" (Weber 1991:175). Troy, a sixteen-year-old Halifax street youth describes what it is like: "It's hard to go to school and be on the streets. I had to take a year off school to adapt to street life because it was hard and all these things hit you at once . . . you have to do everything on your own." Moreover, many related aspects combine to worsen the street youth's experiences with educational systems:

> Their difficulties with learning typically began years ago in elementary school where teachers and caregivers failed to recognize their struggles with the curriculum and consequently failed [to] supplement their educational experience with additional tutoring and/or special one-on-one attention. These problems worsened in secondary school, where the growing frustration with the difficulties posed by the curriculum led to inappropriate behavior which, in a vicious cycle disrupted their schooling still further through suspension, expulsion, or simple distraction. (Brooks, 1990:22 as quoted in Fitzgerald, 1998)

Many street youth who have been interviewed spoke of their disillusionment with the traditional school. Rather than receiving support and guidance from schools, they functioned like a distant relative, demonstrating a lack of understanding for their unique situations. The majority of street youth have poor academic achievement and a strong dislike for the school environment, their peers, and the curriculum, frequently speaking about "boredom" in the classroom and a sense of "not being able to fit in." According to Michael Fitzgerald's analysis of the educational system and Halifax street youth, "[t]heir deepening sense of isolation, abandonment, inadequacy, frustration, negative identification, failure, and lack of felt understanding or support from others, becomes the everyday material these youth bring to their educational experiences" (1998:26).

Alternatives

Notably, the most successful programs and services tend to employ distinct provisions and environments in working with street youth. Youth shelters and drop-in clinics have been labelled alternative or informal as opposed to formal social service organizations. In her discussion of alternative institutions, Rothschild-Whitt provides a useful definition of informal and alternative organizations as "parallel to, but outside of, established institutions [rational-bureaucracies] and which fulfil social needs (for education, food, medical aid, etc.) without recourse to bureaucratic authority" (1979:509). In essence, many youth shelters are organizations that counter the dominant trends of the conventional welfare state, distinguished by their alternative organizational relations and structures. Ideally, youth shelters are non-bureaucratic, nonprofessional, de-secularized, and decentralized. Their status as direct providers of basic needs services without requiring youth to disclose personal information is that which sets them apart from the mainstream. Moreover, youth shelters often have roots in religious and in classical charity, characterized by simple organizational structures that provide immediate services in a flexible, caring, and easily accessed environment. In general, alternative/informal agencies tend to have the following characteristics: innovation, flexibility, participation, protector of particularistic interests, and providers of immediate needs not met generally by formal structures (Kramer, 1981).

Conversely, established child welfare institutions in North and South America, according to many authors, have failed to help those on the streets. This failure is considered to be a direct result of the very character of the conventional welfare system as a "professional-machine-bureaucracy" that is based on intense information gathering, record keeping and rehabilitation, and which is rigidly organized around and dependent upon efficiency of service outputs (Henry, 1987). The youth shelter, in contrast, emerged out of the ideals of the Settlement movement and according to its advocates, is presently the only organization that is simple and flexible enough to respond to hard to reach populations (such as the homeless) through the provisions of food, shelter, and clothing to "all who come."

Formal and alternative social service agencies make different assumptions about the nature of problems and the ways to deal with them. The relationships between service providers and youth clients, and the organizational set-up in which help occurs, are but two problematic areas that receive different organizational approaches. Since most alternative agencies arise in response to lack of available services or perceived inadequacy of existing services, their domain is more narrowly defined than the formal child welfare system by focusing upon a specific population or set of needs. Additionally, service technologies differ for both groups. Formal agencies rely on intervention strategies based upon scientific knowledge (rationalized measures of effectiveness and efficiency) and administered by professionals through structured interactions between clients and staff, where control of form and content lies with the professional. Informal agencies on the other hand tend to rely upon client experience and participation as the predominant mode of intervention and rationale for activity, engaging fewer (if any) professionals, and pursuing egalitarian relationships between participants and staff (Gidron and Hasenfeld, 1994). Moreover, alternative agencies are regularly characterized by horizontal personal relationships, interchangeability of roles, diffusion of authority, and by participatory and democratic structures with few rules. In contrast, formal agencies are regularly characterized by bureaucratic structures that are reinforced by hierarchical relations, a reliance upon professionals, and by little client input. According to Henry (1987):

> The main conclusion which can be drawn from the characteristics and the general scene of homelessness is that the response of voluntary shelter organizations to the problem of homelessness is antithetical to the response of

the professional bureaucracy. As such, it lacks the discipline and authority, the orderliness, the predictability, the standardized solutions and technologies of the accepted bureaucracy and the social work profession. (145)

According to Berman and West (1995), however, nonprofit organizations do have legitimacy in working with homeless populations because they provide a forceful voice on behalf of this marginalized population and are quick to respond to crises (237). In a national survey of nonprofit organizations serving homeless populations in the United States, Berman and West view voluntary shelters (and other nonprofit agencies) as an "important driving force" in solving the homeless crisis. Precisely, alternative organizations tend to be "mission-oriented" and promoters of a more humanistic welfare state (Lipsky and Smith, 1989–90). The emergence of shelters for street youth along with other alternative social service organizations such as drop-ins, soup kitchens, detoxification centers, independent and cooperative housing and health clinics, all represent disparate public efforts to respond to youth homelessness in its complexity. Often, the formal system of child care and protection with its top-down structure of delivery has been described, by many in the alternative camp, as part of the problem.

The informal system has been repeatedly described in the human service delivery literature as favorable to the formal child welfare institution, because it provides environments for homeless youth that are more conducive to personal healing and growth. Lipsky and Smith explain the qualitative difference between the two systems accounting for the disparity in the levels of success experienced by each:

> First, if people say they are hungry, or homeless, or recently assaulted and fearful for their safety, nonprofit [voluntary] organizations are inclined to accept such testimony as sufficient. Government officials upholding the equity requirement cannot tolerate such an accepting attitude. (1989–90:632)

Increasingly, scholars and researchers portray the formal child welfare system as a bureaucratic, machine-like apparatus that is cold and rigid, responsible for perpetuating street life for many young people.

Street-kid shelters proliferated in the 1970s and 1980s due to the growing number of runaways and street kids in need of a safe refuge.[4] Aleva (1988) and Karabanow (1999a; 2000; 2004a) suggest that these shelters have been portrayed as alternatives for youth who mistrusted traditional services:

Runaway children tended to be mistrustful of adults and adult organizations and institutions. The youngsters seemed to be seeking a better social environment than those in their own homes and their communities, and avoided assistance from the traditional social welfare agencies which they regarded as too structured, too impersonal or too inflexible to respond to their own problems or needs. (Saltonstall, 1973 quoted in Alleva, 1988:29)

Consequently, the alternative youth shelter, expressing a certain degree of dissatisfaction with the inadequate methods and resources plaguing the public welfare system, emerged to supplement (extend) and complement (add something qualitatively different to) the formal child welfare system.

Mapping what works

A general consensus now exists within the social work literature about what "doesn't work" with street youth (see for example Karabanow and Clement, 2004). The following discussion draws upon lessons from the field by way of exploring "what works" in terms of how some organizations have been successful in attracting challenging street youth. Here I focus specifically on the organizational tenets of alternative service providers, which promote social justice and anti-oppressive philosophies of practice and of overall operation.[5] Organizations successful in attracting street youth appear to promote locality and social development, active participation, structural definition and analysis of individual situations, consciousness raising and action. After completing an overview of much of the extant research regarding street children today, Earls and Carlson suggest that "more systematic analyses of the services available to street and working children must be obtained" (1999:75) in order to enhance our understanding of best practice approaches. My aim here is to identify the primary characteristics of street youth organizations that appear to "work best" for service users.[6]

Locality development

Locality development encompasses the spirit of grass root cultivation—the notion of a "bottom-up" approach to institutional organization. More specifically, locality development takes into account a locality's definition of the phenomenon under study, its direction for intervention, as well as its

distinctive involvement in the implementation of programs and their sus-
tainability. Because street youth require basic services that can be administered in a timely, flexible, and caring manner, a significant dimension of locality development is its proffering of immediate responses to problems in
a caring, sensitive, and compassionate manner (Karabanow, 2004a). Youth
who approach social service agencies for shelter, medical services, showers, food, and clothing often attempt to avoid at the same time those organizations that maintain obtrusive rules and regulations. Toronto's Covenant
House (CH), Guatemala's Casa Alianza (CA), Halifax's ARK and Phoenix
Youth Services, and Montreal's Dans La Rue (DLR) are alternative street
youth services which advocate immediate attention to the needs of their
clients. For instance, prior to any type of intake procedure, workers at
these centers are trained to identify emergency concerns of clients such as
the need for food, clothing, sleep, a shower, or medical attention.

Moreover, locality development assumes the creation of a symbolic
space (Karabanow, 1999a; 2003)—a place where marginal populations
might feel safe and respected. As a seventeen-year-old Montreal street girl
eloquently noted: "[DLR] cares about you, they really care . . . the staff
treat you like you're their family." The youth organizations that are popular are those which transform into "surrogate families" (Karabanow and
Rains, 1997; Ruddick, 1996) for street youth, presenting an environment
where one's ideas, thoughts, and experiences are listened to and valued:

> Claire [worker] actually, she's like all of our [street youth] mothers, she does
> so much for us. Actually next week she's setting me up with a free dental ap-
> pointment to fix a chipped tooth. (Abe, Age 18, Toronto)

> If I was having a real bad day or something, I would probably go right to ARK
> and speak with Joanne [a staff member], or else I would go to Phoenix and
> speak with Liz [a staff member] because they are people who care. (Trevor,
> Age 19, Halifax)

Notably, when several Halifax street youth suggested they would be leaving for Montreal, they added that they would be going to DLR because it is
the only dog-friendly shelter in eastern or central Canada:

> I think there's a big problem with facilities being accessible to kids and their
> dogs. In Montreal there's a really large facility [DLR], it's a great place and
> they allow dogs and it's great. There's no reason not to accept dogs. They are
> cutting off so many kids by not allowing that because [having a dog is] com-
> panionship, it's security, it's so many things. (Sandra, Age 19, Halifax)

Likewise, similar attitudes were expressed by youth in Guatemala City's CA: "You can be yourself here. You don't have to act all tough like on the street" (Tosi, Age 16).

When basic needs are sufficiently met for the short term, and a sense of care, trust, and respect emerges between parties, young people experience a more positive community atmosphere. Ultimately, alternative agencies for street youth attempt to create a liaison with hard-core populations by first providing them with basic services, by enabling them to feel safe, cared-for, and "a part of something." This primary mission of alternative shelters is underscored by the one Halifax youth's observations that shelter workers have been the only positive force in his street life career, and that they are the only people with whom he feels comfortable speaking to about personal issues: "I like the people that work here [shelter], I really do, and they've been here for me twice now. Some of them are just really friendly; you make friendships here with them, so they're easy to talk to" (Carter, Age 21, Halifax).

Locality development provides a foundation for street youth to build a sense of place, frequently enabling the development and first-time experience of community for many vulnerable youth. A place where one might feel safe, cared for and accepted, is a unique phenomenon for most street youth: ". . . This [CH] is the only home I got" (Steven, Age 17, Toronto). Toronto's CH, for instance, places a lot of attention on the cleanliness of the shelter because within their purview a clean house equates to feelings of respect and personal dignity for street youth, as it might for anyone. Montreal's DLR gained an impressive reputation among hard core street youth because the agency provides flexible, unobtrusive services twenty-four hours a day in an ongoing caring, loving, and informal way (see Karabanow, 1999a). The founders of DLR spent much time with street youth ("on the street") discovering their most important needs and idiosyncrasies. Not surprisingly, it metamorphosed from a mobile outreach program housed within a van, to a comprehensive emergency shelter and drop-in service due to its success in identifying the most pressing needs of and gaps in services for street youth. Similarly, many of the nonprofit alternative street youth services in Guatemala, such as Casa Alianza, The Center for Integral Community Development (CEDIC) and Solo Para Mujer, have also created settings where youth can obtain immediate services within a safe, warm, and clean environment—a real difference from the squalor of street life. These non-government organizations in Guatemala have had relative successes in working with street youth in settings characterized by impoverished economies, massive levels of poverty, high levels of illiteracy and malnourishment, and oppressive military political systems. Despite such a bleak environment, the alternative street youth service system has provided at-risk and street entrenched adolescents with places of safety.

Locality development allows for the seeds of community to be planted within the service environment itself, in which the shelter is situated on the front lines, frequently providing first, and consequently, vital contacts for youth in trouble. "What lights up the world and makes it bearable is the feeling which we usually have of our links with it—and more particularly of what joins us to other people" (Halladay 1992:3).

Social development

The notion of social development within an alternative service paradigm recognizes the importance of human capital as well as economic resources in addressing social ills. This approach acknowledges the strength of individual and collective explorations, analyses, and solutions to crises. As such, a social development perspective adopts a humanistic and holistic approach to an individual and their situation—confronting simultaneously the myriad social, political, and economic forces which shape understandings of issues like youth homelessness. For example, social justice and anti-oppressive organizations do not identify an individual through her or his unconventional street behaviors. Rather than naming someone a "prostitute" or "drug addict," from within a social development paradigm the aim is to gain an understanding of individual identities as complex personal and political constructs that are unfixed and ever-changing. Montreal's DLR, for example, places much attention upon providing youth with individual and group supports within a strength-based perspective. Through strategies of mutual aid and self-help, counseling and intervention tactics become resilient activities that are empowering for both workers and youth. The fundamental elements necessary for fostering social development include: support and guidance with skills building and sharing (e.g., preparing for a job interview; creating a résumé; searching for housing); allowing participants to realize that they are not alone in their predicaments (i.e., forging community space); and teaching that one's personal strengths, when linked to those of others in similar and/or different situations, can be highly effective in the search for solutions. Additionally, youth learn to value and respect themselves and others, acknowledging their agency and resolve in past, present, and future endeavors. For example, Toronto's CH places much attention on the resident's acceptance of his or her situation, and on taking individual responsibility for one's past and future possibilities. Accordingly, the hope is for youth to learn to take control of their lives, to place themselves in the "driver seat," by choosing directions, and making choices: "I realize more now that I can change things, things in my life that I don't like . . . one of the things I learned [at DLR]" (Sylvia, Age 15, Montreal).

Fundamentally, anti-oppressive organizations foster an individual's strengths and acknowledge the significance of one's personal experiences in the processes of identity formation. A telling example of this type of modus operandi comes from DLR. For instance, after several weeks of re-gaining their strength and feeling more comfortable within their new sur-rounding, five street youth asked the agency whether they could use a downstairs office to discuss amongst themselves certain issues, such as re-counting their lives prior to moving onto the street, their consequent experiences once on the street, and what plans they held for the future. Along with one worker who had created a close relationship with this group, a mutual-aid, self-help site was born. This informal group, which was led by street youth with a worker acting solely as a guide or enabler, functioned as a secure forum for the sharing of personal experiences and knowledge. In the end, participants left this group with a greater sense of self-confidence, realizing they were not alone, and that there existed positive options with which to solve many of their difficult problems (Karabanow, 1999a). At DLR and CA, group activities impact the power of collective responses to trauma (such as abuse and street-related criminal behavior). Ultimately, a social development model upholds a holistic approach to a person's situation and accounts for the multiple and intersecting dimensions that con-tribute to an individual's reality. The complex nature of problems asso-ciated with street living and which are best addressed using a holistic approach is exemplified in what this Halifax street youth has to say about his personal and numerous struggles:

> You go through ten years of not having a job and living on the street. Becom-ing employed is more difficult than just having the motivation to get up and get out there and do the job interview and whatnot. You may not have any clothes, which some agencies can help you with and then there is the whole self-esteem thing, that's what screws me a lot of the time when I'm trying to

get off the street. I don't have any self esteem left anymore. I get to a certain point and I get to what I call "fuck it." "You know, this isn't going to work, I'm just going to screw it up, I never do anything right, fuck it!" (Tony, Age 22, Halifax).

The group dynamic that is part and parcel of the holistic approach underscores individual agency in understanding, accepting and addressing traumatic experiences within a collective environment. Casa Alianza in Guatemala City has created, for instance, a supportive venue where youth take the time to reflect on past, present, and future issues, while connecting with others in a safe environment. While local development lays the groundwork for future initiatives taken by participants, social development enables youth to feel a sense of belonging, to see themselves not as street runaways but as citizens dealing with difficult circumstances.

Active participation

A key tenet of both locality and social development is the authentic (rather than token) youth involvement in an organization's operations. Montreal's DLR exemplifies this approach by involving street youth in the design and implementation of shelter programs (Karabanow, 1999a). In fact, the shelter which is called the "Bunker" received its name from a committee of street youth, and many residents sit on committees responsible for the development and implementation of DLR service policy. Moreover, positions responsible for self-help/mutual-aid groups, peer mentoring, and cooking within the organization also incorporate street youth in service provision.

Active participation within the alternative service organization can also entail establishing links to the many different aspects of mainstream culture. An important part of developing a sense of community, and of feeling oneself to be an active citizen, is the need for youth to form positive relations with the world outside of the shelter. It is imperative for agencies working with hard-core and marginalized populations to redirect them toward mainstream culture, while helping them to develop the necessary skills and attitudes to negotiate life in the mainstream. In many Third World countries, where economic developments are often impeded by global relations of power that favor the industrialized world, bike courier projects have been established through the work of Toronto's Street Kids International (SKI) with the cooperation of local Third World business groups. In these bike courier projects street children act as messengers between business communities. An important outcome of this project has been the creation of positive connections between the street children and mainstream societies of the participating countries; connections which permit feelings of being a worthy part of a productive (business) community, and which allow for previously unforeseen opportunities of potential employment. Moreover, organizers of the bike courier projects have noted an increase in participants' self-worth, self-esteem and confidence (Dalglish, 1998).

In a similar vein, Toronto's CH has forged collaborative educational and work programs with local universities and businesses in order to provide street youth with job training outlets, apprenticeship programs, and learning projects. Numerous participants have subsequently been employed by the collaborating partners. Montreal's DLR has also fostered constructive relations with local universities, police, neighborhood businesses, and community centers by way of providing street children with opportunities to familiarize themselves with their community, and to utilize its available resources and facilities. In addition, collaborative relationships also provide street youth and their communities with the potential for greater awareness and appreciation of one another. Weekly baseball games, for example, involving a local police station and street youth in Montreal allowed for positive interactions between these two groups that have been traditionally fraught with conflict and misinformation. Yet another strategy that is used by many shelters entail volunteers from mainstream organizations who spend time working with youth around educational upgrading, computer training, life skills, and mentoring, to name only a few of the possible types of volunteer-directed activities. A youth in Halifax describes the support he obtained at a shelter while attending school: "It works out excellent [being at school] because there are volunteer people [at the shelter] who take the time out of their day to come in and help us with our homework" (Nicko, Age 19).

The Center for Integral Community Development (CEDIC), a rural Guatemalan prevention program, has created numerous micro-enterprises and small loan projects that help indigenous families link their skills to the local market place. CEDIC has also developed impressive apprenticeship programs for children in the agriculture, manufacturing, and information sectors. Needless to say, such programs provide street children, and adults in the case of Guatemalan programs, with a sense of belonging to a larger community by integrating them into their local environments, and by providing the assistance needed to become productive citizens.

Linking with the "outside world" allows street youth to lead "normalized" lives, and to break away from unconventional and, in particular, unproductive, not to mention, dangerous, subcultures. At the same time, however, organizations should not ignore some of the unique and positive elements of street culture such as individual strength of character related to street survival and group solidarity.

One unintended shortcoming of traditional street youth services stems from the designation of youth participants as clients or consumers, which has the effect of further alienating some participants. The goal of social service agencies must be to reintegrate street youth into mainstream culture, while signaling the importance of their unique and alternative attributes. This orientation is a delicate balance between street ethics and mainstream culture's values. For example, DLR collaborated with a recycling company to create a job-training program that successfully fused positive street-related values, such as environmentalism and advocacy, with mainstream values, such as bottom-line business principles. While obtaining such a delicate balance can prove difficult, allowing youth to participate in creating such a balance can be helpful. Many street youth dream of traditional careers such as teaching, marketing, computer programming, and law, for example, yet seek unique paths to obtaining such employment. Much like a parent watching their adolescent choose her or his path of discovery, agencies need to be patient, supportive, and provide guidance, so that youth might attempt to create their own fusion between alternative street cultures and mainstream culture.

Active participation, notwithstanding the associated difficulties of implementation and coordination (see Cameron and Karabanow, 2003), allows for youth to experience acceptance and belonging. Moreover, many youth perceive involvement as a way to "pay back" organizations to which they feel a sense of commitment and loyalty. As one Montreal street youth commented: "I don't mind getting up early for these meetings [at DLR]; I owe them at least that much; they were there when I really needed somebody" (Barrie, Age 19). As such, participation in operational matters of alternative organizations is commonly equated by youth with acceptance and respect. Many adolescents perceive participation as "being needed" and "feeling worthy." In this sense, active participation represents for street youth a form of partnering, where both workers and residents join together to build a common vision and direction for the organization.

Structural definition of situation

Much of the current mainstream street youth literature has highlighted both the "push" factors, some examples of which are poverty, family dysfunction, abuse, school problems, and the "pull" factors, examples of which are independence, freedom, drug/alcohol abuse, that inform discussions of street youth etiology. Much of this debate revolves around individual pathology and structural forces (i.e., are street youth a problem of social misfits or social structure?). Social justice and anti-oppressive organizations adopt the latter vision, believing that political, economic, and social forces propel the individual toward street life. Understanding the "whole" person entails a holistic perspective of both individual traits and structural constraints. For example, DLR acknowledges that most youth exist on the street due to a lack of both affordable and clean housing and adequate employment. As such, rather than blaming the individual, DLR links political and economic forces to the individual's present situation. Moreover, organizations such as DLR, CA, ARK, Phoenix and CH acknowledge the myriad of street activities (both legal and illegal) undertaken by youth in order to survive. Rather than condemning illegal street behavior, anti-oppressive organizations place them within a larger context of exploitation and victimization. As a CH front line worker explained, "I don't see these kids as male hustlers or female hookers; that would make them delinquents. Rather, I see them as young boys and girls exploited and taken advantage of by our society" (David, Toronto). In this sense, anti-oppressive organizations' assessments of street youth complement street youth's self-constructed images—fostering "value/identity harmony"—which might lead to meaningful interaction. Several street youth highlight this perspective:

> CH treats me well, not like I'm some dumb hooker . . . it's like what a family should be. (Lana, Age 19, Toronto)

> I came here [CA] because it's the only place that cares, I got a clean bed, good food . . . workers are really nice. . . . (Miguel, Age 15, Guatemala)

> The staff don't judge you here [DLR], you can tell them whatever . . . like my stuff with jail and all and they [DLR staff] listen. . . . (Jay, Age 18, Montreal)

Along with a sense of community, street youth also find refuge in sites where they are accepted for who they are, and also deemed to be worthy citizens. This unique contemporary environment contrasts sharply with the prevalent public perceptions of street youth as "street urchins," "bums," and "dregs of society" that are deeply rooted in traditional charity-based social work and welfare reform of the nineteenth and early twentieth centuries.

Consciousness raising

Enabling interaction within a safe setting allows for genuine explorations of an individual's past and present experiences and future goals. At their own choosing, residents of DLR engage in a sort of cathartic enterprise, usually within an informal mutual aid group, where youth can connect their experiences to those of others as well as engage in deeper understandings of specific issues. On numerous occasions, I have witnessed the epiphanies of others; the moment in which a young person realizes that her or his history of family abuse not only mirrors street youth colleagues, but also raises doubt as to his/her culpability (or more apt, self-blame) regarding past acts (Karabanow, 1999a). Moreover, accepting this new reality also allows for a reconsideration of present survival activities (such as prostitution). Consciousness raising implies an intimate and in-depth exploration into one's actions through a process of knowledge building, solidarity and commitment. Halifax's ARK drop-in clinic engaged participants in the making and disseminating of a documentary depicting the "truer" (or more accurate) experiences of squeegee youth. Part of this process involved critical reflection—linking one's situation to micro and macro intentions. At Guatemala's CA, there is a strong movement (involving street youth and the organization) to pressure glue manufacturers to change the way in which they sell products that ultimately end up in the hands of street youth. Youth learn to connect their addictions not only to past and present struggles in their own lives, but also the economic and political culture which allows for corporate revenues to supersede social responsibility.

Consciousness raising emerges as an intimate process of accepting, exploring, and ultimately reconstructing one's past, present, and future orientations. Through individual and collective enterprises, anti-oppressive organizations foster safe community settings where individuals can build and rebuild a sense of identity, worth, and understanding of their immediate environments.

Social action

Apart from allowing youth to feel comfortable and cared for, many anti-oppressive organizations also move a step further—advocating for and on behalf of alienated and stigmatized populations. Social action implies a commitment to fundamental change in the form of demands for increased resources and/or equal treatment. As such, social action involves consciousness raising made active and public—allowing those without a voice to be heard through critical reflection and empowerment strategies. DLR has many examples of social action endeavors—including, joining with street youth to protest the closing of a local park; petitioning municipal and provincial leaders for increased youth employment and affordable housing; and, facilitating a group of youth (named "Punk Not Junk") to mobilize the street youth community in order to sensitize the public as to the actual experiences of street life and heroin ("junk") abuse (Karabanow, 1999a). Along the same lines as Gustavo Guttierrez's liberation theology, social action highlights a joining of forces among service providers and service users in order to voice common struggles. The process of social action appears to grow out of a culmination of previous tenets highlighted in this paper. To reach social action, a sense of commitment and trust needs to be forged between actors—fostered in settings where locality and social development (i.e., community building) are fused with active participation, structural analyses, and consciousness raising. In Guatemala, CA has been a leader in raising awareness of the horrific treatment of street youth at the hands of paramilitary forces. In addition, the organization has developed a legal department to build court cases against involved parties. CA staff and street youth advocates have been threatened, terrorized, and even murdered in their struggle to bring guilty individuals to trial. In a vastly different political and economic climate, Toronto's CH has been prominent in advocating government bodies for higher per diem rates to house street youth. Moreover, the shelter has joined with street youth to protest recent conservative government housing and welfare policies. Such examples signify the alliance between social justice/anti-oppressive organizations and marginalized populations in fighting for legitimacy, respect, and tangible resources.

While locality and social development can be interpreted as activities focused upon process issues (i.e., building community), social action initiatives are largely interested in end results (i.e., gaining resources). Maintaining both avenues of service delivery can provide organizations with comprehensive, committed, and complementary approaches to social justice/anti-oppressive practice.

Conceptual frameworks

There are numerous "conceptual maps" informing the manner by which services for street youth are delivered. For example, some agencies adopt family reconciliation frameworks, others espouse "tough love" perspectives, while still others maintain outreach goals (Karabanow and Clement, 2004). Lusk (1989), Carizosa and Poertner (1992), and Rizzini and Lusk (1995) outline four overarching ideological assumptions that guide service provision for street youth. First, the "correctional and institutional" approach views young people on the street as "delinquents" and "threats to community safety" and thus intervention follows the ideology of removal from society and correction of personal pathologies. This response tends to blame the individual for being a street youth or engaging in street activity (such as drugs and prostitution). The "rehabilitation" approach is more benevolent than the correctional approach, yet it still assumes personal pathology or deficiencies. Within this approach, street youth are perceived as inadequate, needy, abandoned, or harmed. The intervention involves protection and rehabilitation—attempting to "fix" the individual and integrate him/her back into society. The third approach is that of "street education," which assumes that street youth are normal adolescents who have been forced by a deficient society to live under difficult conditions. In other words, street youth are in their predicament because of structural social deficiencies (such as lack of affordable housing and meaningful employment). In order to fight the problem, this approach argues that education and empowerment of street youth will lead to engaged collective action whereby solutions to collective problems can be forged. The last approach identified is "prevention" and involves strategies of education and advocacy in order to find solutions to the root causes of homelessness. This approach attempts to stop young people from moving toward street life, and rather than focusing upon institutionalized strategies, it promotes community-based programs (such as after-school programs and midnight basketball activities).

Agencies and programs that have shown remarkable success in attracting street youth have overwhelmingly adopted "street education" and "prevention" strategies. The major characteristics of such initiatives include: providing for basic needs (such as shelter, food, clothing) in an immediate fashion; fostering the strengths of participants through community building; linking with external communities; building true participation; allowing for consciousness raising, and, advocating on participants' behalves. When interrelated, these elements function to create a safe and caring environment where participants can build an empowered and resilient community. In other words, when taken together, these elements forge a "culture of hope" for an otherwise marginalized and forgotten population. Once these elements are in place, they can produce a synergistic environment whereby community is expanded and renewed.

CHAPTER SIX

Conclusion

Nobody deserves to live on the streets . . .
Nicko, 19, Halifax

Resilience and courage

Street youth populations are not homogeneous. The street lives of youth are distinguished by many features including age, sexual orientation, race, gender, ethnicity, and prior "pushes" to street life. The aim of this analysis has been two-fold: to stress the importance of understanding how characteristic differences shape street careers, and to trace and document what were sometimes surprisingly similar themes across economic, political, and cultural divides, by drawing together data from a number of diverse contexts. My research has revealed, for instance, that the majority of street youth in the three Canadian cities of Toronto, Montreal, Halifax, as well as those in Guatemala City in Latin America, have all fled traumatic, abusive or, at the very least, unhealthy family situations. Additionally, more than half of the street youth surveyed in this study have experienced problematic child welfare interventions which have served only to further worsen their individual situations. The streets, therefore, have become a kind of safe haven for many within the street youth population of those cities, despite the multiple dangers which characterize life of the streets.

As evidenced in Chapter Four, young people navigate through street culture by moving in and out of interactions with mainstream culture, human service organizations as well as illegal and unconventional activity, in order to survive. What is immediately clear amidst the turmoil of life on the streets is the resilience and creativity of street youth regarding their needs for shelter, food, clothing, employment, and, for many, the negotiations involved in opening the way for healthier and safer lives. The various stages of street life engagement and disengagement involve a degree of self-awareness on the part of the street youth. How an individual feels about herself, how she conceives of escape from difficult situations, how she perceives strategies for day-to-day survival, how she envisions different paths away from the street and, ultimately, how she embarks upon new journeys and scripts new and ever-changing identities, are all processes in which street youth demonstrate varying degrees of thoughtfulness and reflexivity.

The desire and will to survive in the face of adversity are reflected in the individual commitments to make sense of variable and frequently unpredictable environments, to cope with the after effects of past and ongoing struggles, and to construct personal objectives, no matter how minor in scale they might be. It is essential for all, but especially for those who work with street youth, to understand that street youth respond best within relationships informed by compassion and respect. We need to recognize the unique circumstances which inform and shape the lives of youth who end up on the streets searching for security and love among many other basic necessities. Street youth are not "social misfits" plagued by personal pathologies. For the majority, street life is the only viable alternative to extremely problematic (or nonexistent) family or child welfare settings.

Alternative systems

Within the last twenty years, there has been an increase in the number of alternative, nongovernment agencies working with homeless youth. Generally, these agencies have emerged out of a frustration toward the formal child welfare system, a system that has been consistently characterized as bureaucratic, institutional, and having too many roadblocks which prevent the immediate delivery of much needed services. Scientific studies and reports abound with accounts of hard-core street youth being ignored, neglected, misunderstood, or harmed rather than helped by formal systems (Alleva, 1988; Edney, 1988; Henry, 1987; Lave, 1995; Human Rights Watch, 1997; Karabanow, 2000; 2002). The requirements to receive attention and gain access to needed services within formal systems are unrealistic and do not take into account the absence of convention in the lives of street youth which make it difficult for street youth to make mandatory appointments, call back at specific times, provide a phone number and fixed address, and to disclose personal information or provide identification.

At the same time, precisely because alternative agencies are alternative, frequently operating outside of any governmental auspices, they are comparatively small, non-bureaucratic, rather flexible, not so rigidly professional—acting as "buffers" (Vosburgh, 1988) for hard-to-serve populations vis-à-vis the formal system. Generally, alternative service agencies are viewed as respectful and caring places where street youth are able to regain their lost sense of humanity and personal dignity. Alternative agencies provide a "culture of hope" and, as a result, have had greater success in attracting disenfranchized and marginalized youth. Organizations like the ones in this research (Dans La Rue, Covenant House, Street Kids International, ARK, Phoenix Youth Services, The Center for Integral Community Development, and Casa Alianza) are prime examples of agencies and programs that have reached out to street youth in innovative ways.

Some of the common attributes of these agencies include: immediate and direct service provision; developing safe, trustful, and respectful relationships with children; working to join street youth to external communities; providing a safe and secure community for young people on the street; developing the competence of street youth circles in order that they can define their own situations and construct their own paths; and, advocating for increased resources and/or equal treatment. As a result, such agencies have functioned as authentic alternative services which have also successfully created "symbolic spaces" in which street youth can imagine new friendships and possibilities, be inspired by fresh dreams and, perhaps most importantly, realize the benefits of acquiring ownership or possession of one's life.

Merging locality development and social action

As we have seen, successful street youth agencies and programs operate within two different yet complementary arenas. In one, an intense focus is placed on locality development, which is understood as broad participation at the grassroots level, and which emphasizes community competence and social integration. Montreal's DLR, Halifax's ARK and Phoenix Youth Services and Toronto's Street Kids International are examples of programs that have re-energized participants by allowing them to feel safe, cared for, and owners of their respective programs. In the other sphere of operation, organizations such as Guatemala's CA and CEDIC, Toronto's CH and Montreal's DLR have adopted social action strategies with the aim of providing street youth with a voice—organizing participants to make demands for increased resources and/or equal treatment. For instance, CA's legal clinic has brought attention to the torture of street youth by military and police regimes. Social action initiatives at DLR involved consciousness raising, mutual aid, and collective responses to such issues as the closing of a downtown park.

Community development and social action operate in a complementary fashion. While social action initiatives focus upon end results (i.e., gaining resources), locality development places importance upon process issues (i.e., the emotional, spiritual, and intellectual needs of a group). In this regard, successful agencies tend to adopt two fundamental roles—that of guide or enabler (i.e., providing resources and information in a supportive and safe environment), as well as the role of partisan (i.e., joining with street youth to protest injustice). It is the fusion of these two roles that have enabled some organizations to be at the vanguard of street youth services.

Lessons from the field

As governments throughout the world distance themselves from important health, education, and social programs, there is an even greater imperative for community-based, alternative organizations to take on the street youth "cause." Increasingly, alternative youth organizations are the providers of basic services and opportunities, the contact point for access to mainstream culture, a source for community building, and advocates for improved living conditions for society's disenfranchised. Street youth services such as Casa Alianza, Covenant House, Phoenix Youth Services, ARK and Dans La Rue have emerged to reorient, redesign and/or to extend a support network for those most marginalized and alienated.

This book has provided some key organizational directives by which to foster a more humane and caring social service delivery system. These characteristics of intervention are becoming imperative for any organization with a mandate to care for the lives of society's marginalized street youth.

Anti-oppressive/social justice organizations allow for the emergence of meaningful and vibrant community settings by embracing grassroot social development, active participation, a structural analysis of the problem, consciousness raising, and social action. These findings can be interpreted as "lessons from the field"—noting what seems to "work best" for hard-core and marginalized street youth populations. Anti-oppressive organizational structures attempt to build safe and respectful environments for marginalized populations. Such findings can hopefully impact the manner by which social work administrators and practitioners understand service delivery within their particular organizational settings, and more specifically, how they conduct meaningful social work within their day-to-day practices.

In the prologue to *When Corporations Rule the World*, David Korten (1995:1) pronounced that "[e]very where I travel, I find an almost universal sense among ordinary people that the institutions on which they depend are failing them." This observation haunts the formal child welfare system. Street youth services such as CH, DLR and CA demonstrate a distinctly different approach to working with street youth, as such, making them significant and "successful" contributors in the lives of street youth.

Notes

Chapter 1

1. I use the term "children" here since street youth in developing countries are much younger than their counterparts in North America. While street youth in Toronto, Halifax and Montreal range from approximately eleven to twenty-two, in Guatemala, they are between seven and thirteen.
2. Both Toronto and Montreal are large metropolitan cities situated in central Canada. Toronto, Ontario, acts as the political and economic hub of Canada while Montreal, Quebec, is considered a cultural and social core which is home to the majority of Canada's francophone population. On the east coast, Halifax, Nova Scotia, is the largest city in the Maritimes and has been primarily a resource-based economic, political, and cultural environment. While Ontario and Quebec are seen as "rich" provinces in terms of economic output, Nova Scotia is considered one of the "poorer" provinces, especially due to the recent depletion of its fishing stock. For diversity, I have included data from Central America's Guatemala City, Guatemala. Situated south of Mexico, Guatemala has experienced a thirty-year long civil war, dictatorial governments, a strong militarized culture, and ravaging poverty. Guatemala (much like Brazil) has become notorious for the existence of large numbers of street children and the horrific treatment of these populations by military and/or paramilitary forces. Even though each of these four sites represents distinct political, economic, and cultural environments, my aim in this book is to present common themes emerging in North America concerning street youth populations, and to employ data from Guatemala as an extreme case comparison and as a warning as to what could soon emerge in the West.
3. Two empirical studies of adult homelessness (McChesney, 1987; Susser, Streuning, and Conover, 1987) found at least one quarter of their populations experienced homelessness as adolescents.

Chapter 2

1. This discussion will center around homelessness as defined in its colloquial meaning: "without home" and will not involve "informal" homeless populations who through ingenuity and improvisation (i.e. "doubled up" families; staying with friends; living in squats) have eluded much social science research.
2. The current social service system can be seen as a re-creation of a previously well established safety net of mental institutions, missions, soup kitchens, and skid row stores that were dismantled by Lyndon B. Johnson's Great Society.
3. All three settings (which developed one from the other) espoused three major philosophies: work, punishment, and deterrence (Baum and Burnes, 1993:100).
4. Questions concerning how to help the homeless have invariably depended on socially constructed definitions of who is worthy of assistance and who is not.
5. The Child Welfare League of America (1991) posited that by 1990 families with young children were the fastest growing segment of the homeless population constituting one third of this group.
6. A Child Welfare League of America (1991) colloquium specifically focused on the link between homelessness and adequate housing. Similarly, a 1990 United States Conference of Mayors discussed the multiple factors that lead to homelessness including lack of affordable housing, poverty, and unemployment (Child Welfare League of America, 1991:1).
7. Baum and Burnes (1993) divide the homeless into those who are temporary (due to single event—10%–20%), episodic (30%—drifting in and out of homelessness) or chronic (homeless for a considerable time—50%) homeless.
8. Even though the public's perception of the homeless person has presently shifted toward viewing him/her as more deserving, we have not changed the way in which we deal with them (which I explore in the shelter section).
9. As Teeter (1995) notes, street youth in urban centers such as New York were shipped to more rural-like settings via "orphan trains" in order to escape cultures of perceived delinquency and crime. Many youth were sent to towns and farm communities in the underpopulated mid-west.
10. Pfohl (1977) notes that by the 1960s, child intervention became "child saving" as opposed to "society saving" primarily due to the revelation of the child victim and adult abuser.
11. See Wilkinson's ethnography of street youth in the North Western United States (1987:23).
12. This debate has been seen in two Canadian newspapers—*The Toronto Star* (Jan. 13–15, 1998) and *The Globe and Mail* (Nov.4, 1997) around discussions as to the number of mentally ill that make up the homeless population. While antipoverty advocates and a recent study from the Clarke Institute of Psychiatry in Toronto suggest that there is only a small percentage of seriously mentally ill (11%) on the streets, other studies by mental health and hostel workers posit the number to be significantly higher.
13. One added factor presented in Baum and Burnes (1993) analysis is the increased population growth in America due to the baby boom years of 1946 to 1964. This cohort, argue the authors, has created two subclasses of homeless people—those who "lost their minds" within the sixties drug-infused counter-

culture, and an emerging underclass (primarily situated in the urban ghetto) for whom opportunities of good jobs and housing never truly materialized. Homeless and runaway youth tend to come from the latter group.

14. Baum and Burnes (1993) posit that up to 85% of all homeless adults suffer from mental illness, drug and alcohol addiction, or some combination of the three.

15. This point has been made by other authors including Wood, Schlossman, Hayashi, and Valdez (1989:14): "The dire economic plight of homeless families must be viewed in the context of their social isolation and their more severe legacy of personal distress."

16. Shelters have multiplied in the United States exponentially during the 1980s—approximately tripling in number every four years. According to the U.S. Department of Housing and Urban Development (HUD), by 1988, there were 5,400 shelters nationwide with 275,000 beds (HUD, 1989:2). The number of family shelters almost quadrupled during the same time frame (HUD, 1989:6). The same phenomenon is occurring in the 1990s. According to the United Way of Greater Toronto, the number of different people using Toronto hostels grew from 25,009 in 1994 to 28,000 in 1996 (*Globe and Mail*, Nov. 4, 1997).

17. Evidence of the dismal shelter conditions can also be found in the legal arena with the New York City case, *Callahan vs. Carey*, which not only revolved around the right to shelter but also minimal standards of decency for public shelters.

18. Even though this may hold some truth, Jencks (1994:45) notes that fewer than half of the homeless adult population uses free shelters on a given night and it is "hard to believe that eliminating shelters would persuade many homeless drug or alcohol users to spend their limited funds on renting a room." Nevertheless, from a moralistic point of view, providing free shelter is society's obligation to those less fortunate and shelter itself is one of the most basic needs of every human being.

Chapter 5

1. Evidence of a growing treatment orientation towards street youth can be seen in the range of practice approaches used in working with this population, including: psychodynamic perspective; attachment theory; and person-environment transactions (Bronstein, 1996).

2. In contrast to organizations where exchange of services is determined by the market place, people-processing–people-changing organizations (schools, hospitals, shelters) confront a "product" (clients) that is able to react and interact within the organization (Lefton, 1970). As such, a focus upon street youth in shelters is vital to my analysis.

3. In his qualitative study of two homeless shelters in Chicago and Tampa, Timmer (1988) contends that shelters make the distinction between deserving and undeserving based on the cause of one's situation (circumstance versus individual fault). I argue that street youth have increasingly become viewed within the deserving category.

4. Karabanow (2000), Price (1989) and Washton (1974) provide insightful accounts of the evolution of specific street youth shelters.

5. A social justice/anti-oppressive framework involves several key overarching tenets: awareness of the mechanisms of oppression, domination, and injustice; acknowledgment of the structural elements at play in human behavior; acceptance of diversity and difference; recognition of the complexity of power; and, necessity for action (Campbell, 2000).

6. A previous study (Karabanow, 2002) explores organizations that "work best" from the point of view of the organization itself.

Bibliography

Abbott, M. and Blake, G. (1988). An Intervention Model for Homeless Youth. *Clinical Sociology Review*, 6, 148–158.

Adams, G.R., Gulotta, T., and Clancy, M.A. (1985). Homeless Adolescents: A Descriptive Study of Similarities and Differences between Runaways and Throwaways. *Adolescents*, 20, 715–724.

Alleva, F. (1988). Youth at Risk, Systems in Crisis: A Dialogue with Youth Who Needed Shelter. Ph.D. dissertation, Education, Boston University.

Americas Watch and Physicians for Human Rights (1991). *Guatemala: Getting Away with Murder*. New York: Human Rights Watch.

Aptekar, L. (1988). *Street Children of Cali*. Durham and London: Duke University Press.

Baker, R. and Panter-Brick, C. (2000). A Comparative Perspective on Children's "Careers" and Abandonment in Nepal. In C. Panter-Brick and M. Smith (Eds.) *Abandoned Children* (pp. 161–181). Cambridge: Cambridge University Press.

Barak, G. (1991). *Gimme Shelter*. New York: Praeger Publishing.

Baum, A. and Burnes, D. (1993). *A Nation in Denial.* Boulder, CO: Westview Press.

Baxter, E. and Hopper, K. (1981*). Private lives/Public Spaces: Homeless Adults on the Streets of New York City*. New York: Community Service Society.

Becker, H. (1953). Becoming a Marihuana User. *American Journal of Sociology*, 49, 235–242.

Berman, E. and West, J. (1995). Public-Private Leadership and the Role of Nonprofit Organizations in Local Government: The Case of Social Services. *Policy Studies Review*, 14 (1/2), 235–246.

Blau, J. (1992). *The Visible Poor*. New York: Oxford University Press.

Brandon, J. (1974). The Relationship of Runaway Behavior in Adolescence to the Individual's Perceptions of Self, the Environment, and Parental Antecedents. Doctoral dissertation, Psychology, University of Maryland, Maryland.

Bronstein, L. (1996). Intervening with Homeless Youths: Direct Practice without Blaming the Victim. *Child and Adolescent Social Work Journal*, 13(2), 127–138.

Cameron, G. and Karabanow, J. (2003). The Nature and Effectiveness of Program Models for Adolescents at Risk of Entering the Formal Child Protection System. *Child Welfare*, LXXXII (4), 443–474.

Campbell, C. (2000). Congruency in Anti-Oppressive Pedagogy. Unpublished dissertation proposal. Social Work, Memorial University, Newfoundland.

Campfens, H. (1997). *Community Development across the World*. Toronto: University of Toronto Press.

Canadian Council on Social Development (1970). *Transient Youth: Report of an Inquiry in the Summer of 1969*. Ottawa: Canadian Council of Development.

Canadian Council on Social Development (1971). *Youth 1971: An Inquiry into the Transient Youth and Opportunities for Youth Programs in the Summer of 1971*. Ottawa: Canadian Council of Development.

Canadian Paediatric Society (1998). *Getting Street Smart: Re-imagining Adolescent Health Care for Street Youth*. Ottawa: Canadian Paediatric Society.

Casa Alianza (1995). Torture of Guatemalan Street Children: Report to the UN Committee Against Torture, Guatemala City: Casa Alianza.

Cauce, A.M., Paradise, M., Ginzler, J.A., Embry, L., Morgan, C.J., Lohr, Y., and Theofelis, J. (2000). The Characteristics and Mental Health of Homeless Adolescents: Age and Gender Differences. *Journal of Emotional and Behavioral Disorders*, 8(4), 230–239.

Child Welfare League of America (1991). *Homelessness: The Impact on Child Welfare in the '90's*. Washington, DC: Child Welfare League of America, Inc.

Cooper, M.A. (1987). The Role of Religious and Nonprofit Organizations in Combating Homelessness. In R. Bingham, R. Green, and S. White (Eds.) *The Homeless in Contemporary Society* (pp. 130–150). Newbury Park: Sage Publications.

Cuomo, A. (1992). *The Way Home: A New Direction in Social Policy*. New York: New York City Commission on the Homeless.

Dalglish, P. (1998). *The Courage of Children*. Toronto: Harper Collins Publishers Limited.

D'Angelo, R. (1974). *Families of Sand: A Report Concerning the Flight of Adolescents from Their Families*. Columbus: Ohio State University.

De Carrizosa, S.O. and Poertner, J. (1992). Latin American Street Children: Problems, Programmes and Critique. *International Social Work*, 35, 405–413.

De Oliveira, W., Baizerman, M., and Pellet, L. (1992). Street Children in Brazil and Their Helpers: Comparative Views on Aspirations and the Future. *International Social Work*, 35(2), 163–176.

Diversi, M., Filho, N., and Morelli, M. (1999). Daily Reality on the Streets of Campinas, Brazil. In M. Raffaelli and R. Larson (Eds.) *Homeless and Working Youth around the World: Exploring Developmental Issues* (pp. 19–34), San Francisco: Jossey-Bass Publishers.

Drake, R., Osher, F., and Wallach, M. (1991). Homelessness and Dual Diagnosis. *American Psychologist*, 46(11), 1149–1158.

Earls, F. and Carlson, M. (1999). Children at the Margins of Society: Research and Practice. In M. Raffaelli and R. Larson (Eds.) *Homeless and Working Youth around the World: Exploring Developmental Issues* (pp. 72–82). San Francisco: Jossey-Bass Publishers.

Edelbrock, C. (1980). Running Away from Home: Incidence and Correlates among Children and Youth Referred for Mental Health Services. *Journal of Family Issues*, 1, 210–228.

Edney, R. (1988). The Impact of Sexual Abuse on Adolescent Females who Prostitute. In M. Michaud (Ed.) *Dead End* (pp. 25–72). Calgary: Detselig Enterprises Ltd.

Ensign, J. (1998). Health Issues of Homeless Youth. *Journal of Social Distress and the Homeless*, 7(3), 159–171.

Farber, E. and Kinast, C. (1984). Violence in Families of Adolescent Runaways. *Child Abuse and Neglect*, 8, 295–299.

Farrow, J., Deisher, R., Brown, R., Kulig, J., and Kipke, M. (1992). *Homeless and Runaway Youth: Health and Health Needs*. Journal of Adolescent Health, 13, 717–726.

Ferrill, L. (1991). *A Far Cry from Home: Life in a Shelter for Homeless Women*. Chicago: Noble Press.

Fitzgerald, M. (1998). *To Live and Learn: Homeless Youth, Literacy, Education and Career*. Halifax, NS: Phoenix Youth Programs.

Freire, P. (1985). Reading the World and Reading the Word: An Interview with Paulo Freire. *Language Arts*, 61(4), 384–391.

Geber, G.M. (1997). Barriers to Health Care for Street Youth. *Journal of Adolescent Health*, 21, 287–290.

Geertz, C. (1983). *Local Knowledge: Further Essays in Interpretative Anthropology*. New York: Basic Books.

Gidron, B. and Hasenfeld, Y. (1994). Human Service Organizations and Self Help Groups: Can They Collaborate? *Nonprofit Management and Leadership*, 5(2), 159–172.

Globe and Mail, November 4, 1997, Editorial.

Godoy, A. S. (1999). "Our Right Is the Right to Be Killed"—Making Rights Real on the Streets of Guatemala City. *Childhood—A Global Journal of Child Research*, 6(4), 423–442.

Goldmier, J. and Dean, R. (1972). The Runaway: Person, Problem or Situation. Paper presented in the United States Senate Hearings on Runaway Youth before the Subcommittee to investigate Juvenile Delinquency of the Committee on the Judiciary, 92 Congress, 1st session, 233–238. Washington: House of Representatives.

Gounis, K. (1992). The Manufacture of Dependency: Shelterization Revisited. *New England Journal of Public Policy*, 8(1), 685–693.

Green, D. (1998). *Hidden Lives: Voices of Children in Latin America and the Caribbean*. Toronto: Between the Lines.

Halladay, A. (1992). An Apologetics of Hope for Social Work and Social Policy: An Invitation to Dialogue. Unpublished manuscript, Dept. of Social Work. University of Queensland, Australia.

Handler, Joel (1996). Down the Bureaucracy: The Ambiguity of Privatization and Empowerment. Princeton, NJ: Princeton University Press.

Hasenfeld, Y. (1972). People Processing Organizations: An Exchange Approach. *American Sociological Review*, 37, 256–263.

Hertzberg, E. (1992). The Homeless in the United States: Conditions, Typology and Intervention. *International Social Work*, 35, 149–161.

Henry, E.M. (1987). Voluntary Shelters for the Homeless as a Population of Organizations. Ph.D. dissertation, Social Work, Bryn Mawr College.

Hoch, C. and Slayton, R. (1989). *New Homeless and Old: Community and the Skid Row Hotel*. Philadelphia: Temple University Press.

Hoch, C. (1987). A Brief History of the Homeless Problem in the United States. In R. Bingham, R. Green and S. White (Eds.). *The Homeless in Contemporary Society* (pp. 16–32). Newbury Park: Sage Publications.

Hopper, K. (1990). The Ordeal of Shelter: Continuities and Discontinuities in the Public response to Homelessness. *Notre Dame Journal of Law, Ethics and Public Policy*, 4, 301–323.

Human Rights Watch (1997). *Guatemala's Forgotten Children: Police Violence and Abuses in Detention*. New York: Human Rights Watch.

Inciardi, J. and Surratt, H. (1998). Children in the Streets of Brazil: Drug Use, Crime, Violence and HIV Risks. *Substance Use and Misuse*, 33(7), 1461–1480.

Janus, M., McCormack, A., Burgess, A., and Hartman, C. (1987). *Adolescent Runaways—Causes and Consequences*. Lexington, MA: D.C. Heath.

Jencks, C. (1994). *The Homeless*. Cambridge, MA: Harvard University Press.

Jenkins, R. (1971). The Runaway Reaction. *American Journal of Psychiatry*, 128, 168–173.

Jewell, M. L. (1993). "It Don't Make No Sense": An Ethnography of a Homeless Shelter. Ph.D. dissertation, Social Work, Bryn Mawr College, Bryn Mawr.

Karabanow, J. (1994). The Shelter Experience: A Case Study of Street Kid Residents at Toronto's Covenant House. Unpublished M.A. thesis, Sociology, McGill University, Montreal.

———. (1999a). Creating Community: A Case Study of a Montreal Street Kid Agency. *Community Development Journal*, 34(4), 318–327.

———. (1999b). When Caring Is not Enough: An Exploration of Emotional Labour at a Canadian Street Kid Shelter. *Social Service Review*, 73(3), 340–357.

———. (2000). A Place for All Seasons: Examining Youth Shelters and the Youth-In-Trouble Network in Toronto. Ph.D. dissertation, Social Work, Wilfrid Laurier University, Ontario.

———. (2002). Open for Business: Exploring the Life Stages of Two Canadian Street Youth Shelters. *Journal of Sociology and Social Welfare* 29(4), 99–116.

———. (2003). Creating a Culture of Hope: Lessons from Street Kid Agencies in Canada and Guatemala. *International Social Work*.

———. (in press). Becoming a Street Youth: Uncovering the Stages to Street Life. In press at *Journal of Human Behavior in the Social Environment*.

———. (2004a). Making Organizations Work: Exploring Characteristics of Anti-Oppressive Organizational Structures in Street Youth Shelters. *Journal of Social Work, 4(1)* 47–60.

———. (2004b). *Exploring Salient Issues of Street Youth in Halifax, Nova Scotia.* Halifax, Nova Scotia: Report to Human Resources Development Canada.

Karabanow, J. and Clement, P. (2004). Interventions with Street Youth: A Review of the Practice-Research Literature. *Brief Treatment and Crisis Intervention, 4 (1)* 93–108.

Karabanow, J. and Rains, P. (1997). Structure Versus Caring: Discrepant Perspectives in a Shelter for Street Kids. *Children and Youth Services Review,* 19(4), 301–322.

Karabanow, J., Leman, M.C., Leveiller, D., and Prowse, A. (1997). *Zone One: A Case Study of Street Kids in Guatemala* City (film documentary).

Kariel, P. (1993). *New Directions: Stepping out of Street Life.* Alberta: Greenway Press.

Katz, M. (1986). *In the Shadow of the Poorhouse: A Social History of Welfare in America.* New York: Basic Books.

Keigher, S. (1992). Rediscovering the Asylum. *Journal of Sociology and Social Welfare.* 19(4), 177–197.

Kipke, M., Simon, T., Montgomery, S., Unger, J., and Iverson, E. (1997). Homeless Youth and Their Exposure to and Involvement in Violence while Living on the Streets. *Journal of Adolescent Health,* 20(5), 360–367.

Klein, J.D., Woods, A.H., Wilson, K.M., Prospero, M., Greene, J., and Ringwalt, C. (2000). Homeless and Runaway Youths' Access to Health Care. *Journal of Adolescent Health,* 27, 331–339.

Korten, D. (1995). *When Corporations Rule the World.* West Hartford: Kumarian Press.

Kozol, J. (1988). *Rachel and Her Children: Homeless Families in America,* New York: Crown Publishers.

Kramer, R.M. (1981). *Voluntary Agencies in the Welfare State.* Berkeley: University of California Press.

———. (1994). Voluntary Agencies and the Contract Culture: "Dream or Nightmare?" *Social Service Review,* 68, 33–60.

Kufeldt, K. and Nimmo, M. (1987). Youth on the Street. *Child Abuse and Neglect,* 11(4), 531–543.

Kurtz, P.D., Jarvis, S.V., and Kurtz, G.L. (1991). Problems of Homeless Youth. *Social Work,* 36(4), 309–314.

Lave, T. (1995). Breaking the Cycle of Despair: Street Children in Guatemala City. *Columbia Human Rights Law Review,* 27(1), 57–121.

Lefton, M. (1970). Client Characteristics and Structural Outcomes. In W. Rosengren and M. Lefton (Eds.) *Organizations and Clients.* (pp. 17–36). Columbus, Ohio: Charles E. Merrill Publishing Co.

Liebow, E. (1993). *Tell Them Who I Am.* New York: Free Press.

Lipsky, M. (1980). *Street-Level Bureaucracy*. New York: Russell Sage Foundation.

Lipsky, M. and Smith, S.R. (1989–90). Nonprofit Organizations, Government and the Welfare State. *Political Science Quarterly*, 104(4), 625–648.

Lipton, F.R. and Sabatini, A. (1984). Constructing Support Systems for Homeless Chronic Patients. In R. Lamb (Ed.) *The Homeless Mentally Ill: A Task Force Report*. Washington, DC: American Psychiatric Association.

Lipton, F.R., Sabatini, A., and Micheals, P. (1986). Characteristics and Service Needs of the Homeless Mentally Ill. In B.E. Jones (Ed.) Treating The Homeless: Urban Psychiatry's Challenge. Washington, DC: American Psychiatric Press.

Lucchini, R. (1996). The Street and Its Image. *Childhood*, 3, 234–246.

Lusk, M.W. (1992). Street Children of Rio de Janeiro. *International Social Work*, 35, 293–305.

Lusk, M.W., Peralta, F., and Vest, G. (1989). Street Children of Juarez: A Field Study. *International Social Work*, 32, 289–302.

Marquez, P. (1999). *The Street Is My Home: Youth and Violence in Caracas*. Stanford: Stanford University Press.

Matza, D. (1969). *Becoming Deviant*. Englewood Cliffs, NJ: Prentice-Hall.

McCarthy, W. (1990). Life on the Streets. Ph.D. dissertation, Sociology, University of Toronto, Toronto.

McChesney, K.Y. (1987*). Characteristics of the Residents of Two Inner-City Emergency Shelters for the Homeless*. City of Los Angeles, Office of the City Attorney.

Michaud, M. (1989). *Dead End*, Alberta: Detselig Enterprise.

Miller, D., Miller, D., Hoffman, F., and Duggan, R. (1980). *Runaways: Illegal Aliens in Their Own Land*. Westport, CT: Praeger Publishing.

Moncrieff, K. (2001). *What Are Effective Strategies in the Prevention and Treatment of Homelessness? A Review of the Literature*. Hamilton, Ontario: Report for Community Advisory Board on Homelessness in Hamilton.

Morrissette, P. and McIntyre, S. (1989). Homeless Youth in Residential Care. *Social Casework*, 20, 165–188.

Morse, G. (1992). Causes of Homelessness. In M. Robertson and M. Greenblatt (Eds.) *Homelessness: A National Perspective* (pp. 3–17). New York: Plenum Press.

Nelson, K. (1995). The Child Welfare Response to Youth Violence and Homelessness in the 19th century. *Child Welfare*, 74(1), 56–68.

Olson, L., Liebow, E., Mannino, F., and Shore, M. (1980). Runaway Children Ten Years Later. *Journal of Family Issues*, 1, 165–188.

Ortiz de Carrizosa, S. and Poertner, J. (1992). Latin American Street Children: Problem, Programmes and Critique. *International Social Work*, 35, 405–413.

Palenski, J. (1984). *Kids Who Run Away*, Saratoga: R.E. Publishers.

Panter-Brick, C. and Smith, M. (2000). *Abandoned Children*. Cambridge: Cambridge University Press.

Pfohl, S. (1977). The Discovery of Child Abuse. *Social Problems*, 24(3), 310–323.

Platt, A.M. (1969). *The Child Savers*. Chicago: University of Chicago Press.

Price, V. (1989). Characteristics and Needs of Boston Street Youth: One Agency's Response. *Children and Youth Services Review,* 11, 75–90.

Raffaelli, M. (1997). The Family Situation of Street Youth in Latin America: A Cross-National Review. *International Social Work,* 40, 89–100.

Raychaba, B. (1989). Canadian Youth in Care. *Children and Youth Services Review,* 11, 61–73.

Rifkin, J. (1995) *The End of Work: The Decline of the Global Labor Force and the Dawn of the Post-Market Era.* New York: G. P. Putnam's Sons.

Rivlin, L.G. and Manzo, L.C. (1988). Homeless Children in N.Y. City: A View from the 19th Century. *Children's Environment Quarterly,* 5, 26–33.

Rizzini, I. and Lusk, M. (1995). Children in the Streets: Latin America's Lost Generation. *Children and Youth Services Review,* 17(3), 391–400.

Robertson, J. (1992). Homeless and Runaway Youths: A Review of the Literature. In M. Robertson and M. Greenblatt (Eds.). *Homelessness: A National Perspective* (pp. 287–297). New York: Plenum Press.

Rossi, P. (1989). *Without Shelter: Homelessness in the 1980's.* Washington, DC: Twentieth Century Fund.

Rothman, J. (1991) *Runaways and Homeless Youth.* New York: Longman Publishing Group.

Rothschild-Witt, J. (1979). The Collective Organization: An Alternative to Rational Bureaucratic Models. *American Sociological Review,* 44, 509–527.

Ruddick, S.M. (1996). *Young and Homeless in Hollywood.* New York: Routledge.

Scull, A. (1977). *Decarceration: Community Treatment and The Deviant—A Radical View.* Englewood Cliffs, NJ: Prentice-Hall.

Shane, P. (1989). Changing Patterns among Homeless and Runaway Youth. *American Journal of Orthopsychiatry,* 59(2), 208–214.

Snow, D. and Anderson, L. (1993). *Down on Their Luck: A Study of Homeless Street People.* Berkeley: Univ. of California Press.

Snow, K. and Findlay, J. (1998). *Youth in Care in Ontario Speak Out.* Toronto, Ontario: Queen's Printer of Ontario.

Solarz, A. (1992). To Be Young and Homeless. In M. Robertson and M. Greenblatt (Eds.) *Homelessness: A National Perspective* (pp. 275–286). New York: Plenum Press.

Speirs, R. (1998). Now Single Welfare Moms in Cross-Hairs of Spending Cuts. *Toronto Star,* Jan. 20.

Spencer, J. (1994). Homeless in River City: Client Work in Human Service Encounters. *Perspectives on Social Problems,* 6, 29–46.

Stark, L.R. (1994). The Shelter as "Total Institution." *American Behavioral Scientist,* 37, 553–562.

Stierlin, H. (1973). Family Perspectives on Adolescent Runaways. *Archives of General Psychiatry,* 29, 56–62.

Strauss, A. and Corbin, J. (1990). *Basics of Qualitative Research.* Newbury Park, California: Sage Publications Inc.

Street, D., Vinter, R., and Perrow, C. (1966). *Organization for Treatment*. New York: Free Press.

Susser, E., Streuning, E., and Conover, S. (1987). Childhood Experiences of Homeless Men. *American Journal of Psychiatry*, 144, 1599–1601.

Teeter, R. (1995). Pre-school Responses to the 19th-century Youth Crisis. *Adolescence*, 30(118), 291–298.

Tiernan, K., Horn, P., and Albelda, R. (1992) Justice not Charity. *Dollars and Sense*, 179, 12–15.

Timmer, D. (1988). Homeless as Deviance: The Ideology of the Shelter. *Free Inquiry in Creative Sociology*, 16(2), 163–170.

UNICEF (1999). *The State of the World's Children*. Oxford: Oxford University Press.

U.S. Department of Housing and Urban Development (1989). *A Report on the 1988 National Survey of Shelters for the Homeless*. Washington, DC: U.S. Department of Housing and Urban Development.

van der Ploeg, J.D. (1989). Homelessness: A Multidimensional Problem. *Children and Youth Services Review*, 11, 45–56.

Veale, A., Taylor, M., and Linehan, C. (2000). Psychological Perspectives of "Abandoned" and "Abandoning" Street Children. In C. Panter-Brick and M. Smith (Eds.) *Abandoned Children* (pp. 131–145). Cambridge: Cambridge University Press.

Visano, L. (1990). The Socialization of Street Children: The Development and Transformation of Identities. *Sociological Studies of Child Development*, 3, 139–161.

Vissing, Y. and Diament, J. (1995). Are There Homeless Youth in My Community? *Journal of Social Distress and the Homeless*, 4(4), 287–299.

Vosburgh, W. (1988). Voluntary Associations, the Homeless and Hard to Serve Populations—Perspectives from Organizational Theory. *Journal of Voluntary Action Research*, 17(1), 10–23.

Wagner, D. (1993). *Checkerboard Square*. Boulder, CO: Westview Press.

Washton, K. (1974). Running Away from Home. *Journal of Social Issues*, 30(1), 181–188.

Weber, M. (1991). *Street Kids*, Toronto: University of Toronto Press.

Weinreb, L. and Rossi, P. (1995). The American Homeless Family Shelter "System." *Social Service Review*, 69(1), 86–107.

Weinreb, L., Goldberg, R., Bassuk, E., and Perloff, J. (1998). Determinants of Health and Service Use Patterns in Homeless and Low-Income House Children. *Pediatrics*, 102(3), 554–562.

Whyte, W. (1955). *Street Corner Society: The Social Structure of an Italian Slum*. Second Edition. Chicago: University of Chicago Press.

Wilkinson, A.M. (1987). Born to Rebel: An Ethnography of Street Kids. Ph.D. dissertation. School of Education, Gonzaga University.

Wiseman, J. (1970). *Stations of the Lost*. Chicago: University of Chicago Press.

Wood, D., Schlossman, S., Hayashi, T., and Valdez, R.B. (1989). *Over the Brink*. Los Angeles: Assembly Office of Research.

Wright, J.D. (1989) *Address Unknown*. New York: Aldine de Gruyter.

Yablonski, L. (1968). *The Hippie Trip*. New York: Pegasus.

Yates, G., Pennbridge, J., Swofford, A., and Mackenzie, R. (1991). The Los Angeles System of Care for Runaway/Homeless Youth. *Journal of Adolescent Health*, 12, 555–560.

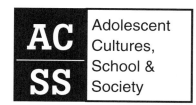

Adolescent
Cultures,
School &
Society

Joseph L. DeVitis & Linda Irwin-DeVitis
GENERAL EDITORS

As schools struggle to redefine and restructure themselves, they need to be cognizant of the new realities of adolescents. Thus, this series of monographs and textbooks is committed to depicting the variety of adolescent cultures that exist in today's post-industrial societies. It is intended to be a primarily qualitative research, practice, and policy series devoted to contextual interpretation and analysis that encompasses a broad range of interdisciplinary critique. In addition, this series will seek to provide a pragmatic, pro-active response to the current backlash of conservatism that continues to dominate political discourse, practice, and policy. This series seeks to address issues of curriculum theory and practice; multicultural education; aggression and violence; the media and arts; school dropouts; homeless and runaway youth; alienated youth; at-risk adolescent populations; family structures and parental involvement; and race, ethnicity, class, and gender studies.

Send proposals and manuscripts to the general editors at:

Joseph L. DeVitis & Linda Irwin-DeVitis
College of Education and Human Development
University of Louisville
Louisville, KY 40292-0001

To order other books in this series, please contact our Customer Service Department at:

(800) 770-LANG (within the U.S.)
(212) 647-7706 (outside the U.S.)
(212) 647-7707 FAX

or browse online by series at:

WWW.PETERLANGUSA.COM